THE CONTRARIAN INSTRUCTOR

LEADING COLLEGE STUDENTS TO ASK AND ANSWER THEIR OWN QUESTIONS

EDUCATION IN A COMPETITIVE AND GLOBALIZING WORLD

EDUCATION IN A COMPETITIVE AND GLOBALIZING WORLD

THE CONTRARIAN INSTRUCTOR

LEADING COLLEGE STUDENTS TO ASK AND ANSWER THEIR OWN QUESTIONS

JOHN WM. FOLKINS

Copyright © 2017 by Nova Science Publishers, Inc.

NOTICE TO THE READER

Library of Congress Cataloging-in-Publication Data

ISBN: 978-1-53611-036-4

Published by Nova Science Publishers, Inc. † *New York*

To my wife, Georgianna

CONTENTS

PREFACE

If you are a college instructor, are your students motivated and able to learn as much as you would like them to learn? Do they readily apply what they have learned? Do they even remember much of it the next semester? Do they ask meaningful questions or are they mostly concerned with asking what will be on the next examination? Are there better ways to reach them? Are there better ways to inspire them to learn more?

It is easy for instructors like me to become entrenched in ways of thinking and teaching approaches that are familiar, effective, and tested within our fields. We may behave conservatively as we are invested in the skills we have developed. We respect the good in the *status quo* and are less likely to take risks with untested ideas or to advocate for untried perspectives. Yet, universities are built on creativity, innovation, and experimentation. Thus, I am up for a challenge. I stand as a contrarian. This book looks at some common and traditional assumptions about college teaching and student learning. Are there better ways to inspire students to learn?

Since the seminal work of Ernest Boyer (1990) over twenty-five years ago, scholars studying teaching and learning have been showing that student-centered instruction can be more effective than traditional methods. Many books have been devoted to this topic and they have taken two general approaches: 1) Some review the scholarly literature and interpret the evidence supporting student-centered instruction. 2) Other books provide explicit procedures and suggestions on how to implement student-centered instruction. Despite these works, many college instructors are still committed to traditional instruction; that is, they concentrate on lecturing and presenting material well rather than on student learning. Here is the problem. Traditional instructors are deeply invested in their methods. The well-known psychological process of *confirmation bias* described in Chapter Six can make them highly skeptical of the existing books reviewing the evidence on student-centered learning. The concern of the traditional instructor is to give an organized and understandable presentation of material. Once that is done, whether the student learns or not is thought to be based on external factors: students do not try, students do not care, students are unprepared, or students do not have the intellectual capacity. Because traditional instructors are not convinced of the need for change, they deem as unnecessary both the books reviewing the literature on student-centered instruction and the books explaining detailed procedures to stimulate it.

The Contrarian Instructor takes a different approach. The literature on the confirmation bias shows that one should not begin with a logical argument. Doing so provokes skeptics to dig in. Instead, one connects with shared values, takes a personal rather than entirely research-based approach, develops concern for a problem, identifies a shared vision for solving the problem, and gives readers ideas for how they can contribute. That is what this book does. It begins with a discussion of scholarly values in liberal education. It uses an informal writing style and invokes personal impressions gathered from my years of experience across a range of disciplines. The book develops a vision for how reflective practice can foster deep learning. Although the book does not take a step-by-step or how-to approach, the latter chapters provide inspiration and direction for how enterprising college instructors can develop their own systems for stimulating deep learning. A powerful aspect of this book is that it is self-reflexive[1]. The book attempts to practice what it preaches.

John Wm. Folkins, Ph.D.
Shallotte, North Carolina

---

[1] It seems like being self-reflective is an obvious construct to use for this book. If I am advocating that an approach works, it would be awkward to then employ a different, less contrarian, style and organization. However, there is also good precedent showing the influential power of being self-reflective, self-replicating, or self-monitoring. See for example, Hofstadter (1985), in which self-reflective sentences are analyzed; examples of such sentences are: This sentence no verb. I am the subject of this sentence. This sentence contradicts itself—or rather—well, no, actually it doesn't!

INTRODUCTION

Our students will learn much more information before going to college than when they are in college. Our students will learn much more information after leaving college than when they are in college. The college experience is only a portion of a student's journey through a life of learning and the central part of college is not leaning facts or information. Yet, college is a tremendous opportunity for students to grow in so many ways. It is a time for them to develop a personal focus for what matters, to sharpen the intellect, and to polish learning skills. That is, it is a time to develop facility at learning that will guide personal interest in probing understanding and meaning in our world. An important principle for maximizing success in college is a contrarian idea: Students should not waste too much time or energy learning information. Information is cheap. On the web, students can find lots of information on virtually everything for virtually nothing. An integral perspective of this book is that college is an opportunity to focus on learning the process of how to learn better. Students should not get sidetracked with too much concern over the specifics of what they are learning.

A second perspective is that students need to develop learning skills for the intrinsic rewards that come with knowing how to learn as effectively as possible. It is a mistake to focus too much on the extrinsic rewards of college like scores and grades that are pursued by strategic learners. Grades might help a student get into graduate or professional school, but generally grades mean little after college. Knowing how to learn is what will be important throughout the rest of the college student's life. Erica Goldson (2010) gave a provocative Valedictorian's address at her commencement from Coxsackie-Athens High School in New York. Zen Pencil has summarized her speech in an enlightening cartoon strip. It is available at: http://zenpencils.com/comic/123-erica-goldson-graduation-speech/. The following is the text from the Zen Pencil cartoon strip. Although the reference is to the student's high school experience, it could apply to college learning as well.

I am graduating. I should look at this as a positive experience, especially being at the top of my class. However, in retrospect I cannot say that I am any more intelligent than my peers. I can attest that I am only the best at doing what I am told and working the system. Yet, here I stand to be proud that I have completed this period of indoctrination. I will leave in the fall to go on to the next phase expected of me, in order to receive a paper document that certifies that I am capable of work. But I contest that I am a human being, a thinker, and adventurer—not a worker. A worker is someone who is trapped within repetition, a slave of the system set up before him. But now, I have successfully shown that I was the best slave. I did what I was told to the extreme.

While others sat in class and doodled to become great artists, I sat in class to take notes and become a great test-taker. While others would come to class without their homework done because they were reading about an interest of theirs, I never missed an assignment. While others were creating music and writing lyrics, I decided to do extra credit, even though I never needed it.

I wonder why did I ever want this position [valedictorian]? Sure, I earned it, but what will come of it? When I leave educational institutionalism, will I be successful or forever lost? I have no clue about what I want to do with my life. I have no interests because I saw every subject of study as work, and I excelled at every subject just for the purpose of excelling, not learning. And quite frankly, now I'm scared.

Chapter 1

THE CONTRARIAN APPROACH
TO COLLEGE STUDENT LEARNING

THE NEED FOR A NEW APPROACH

Years ago when I was a professor at the University of Iowa, I was asked to deliver a guest lecture to a class in a department different from my own. My talk covered the movement of the vocal tract during speech and its related acoustics, an area I knew quite well. I carefully prepared an upbeat presentation with flashy slides. I remember being enthusiastic and the central insights of the lecture fit together into a logical *tour de force*. One couldn't help but be impressed with the material—I thought. The students paid attention. They laughed when they should have laughed. They were entertained. From a traditional perspective, the teaching was quite good.

I ran into a couple of the students a few days later. I asked them what was most interesting or stimulating about my presentation. They said I was nice. They liked me and they had good notes on the presentation. One student then looked away and started to read the newspaper. She would have been looking at a smart phone today. The students may have had notes, but they didn't remember much. From our conversation, I realized that they cared about the material even less. I could dismiss this by claiming that it is hard to reach every student in a large lecture. However, there were less than a half dozen students in the class. I could dismiss this by conjecturing that these students were unprepared or somehow not ready to learn. But this was a class of residents in the Department of Orthodontics. These students had already finished dental school. They were mature students who were industrious and cared deeply about preparing for their future profession as orthodontists. The teaching was good from the point of view of a traditional professor. It was just not relevant enough to make a difference in the lives of the students. The students may have been entertained, but they didn't care about the material in the way that I did. Although I might have tried to explain why what I had to say was important for future orthodontists to know, asserting that the material was important would not have been enough. I had not connected with their value systems. The residents did not have their own questions concerning my material. Their questions were about how the material impacted directly on the practice of orthodontics. I was providing background theory. They wanted specifics related to practice.

As a university administrator for 24 years, I noticed this loss of interest or perhaps inspiration happening during many lectures, even with well-prepared lectures by some of our best instructors. Students are at the lecture because they are expected to be at the lecture. They take notes and they ask what will be on the test. Yet, too often the interest of the professor in the material and the interests of the students are mismatched. A compass for this book is that we must point in a direction that aligns the purposes of the instructor and the educational system with the reasons students have for being in college.

COLLEGE INSTRUCTION AND COLLEGE STUDENT LEARNING

The cover of this book shows a traditional instructor teaching a class of dogs to whistle. The instructor is proud that he has taught the dogs to whistle. Of course, dogs can't whistle, but the professor is not deterred from giving an articulate lecture—it is excellent teaching. The point is that there are two perspectives of instruction, one about teaching and one about learning. Through the first perspective, it is the responsibility of the instructor to present a comprehensive, clear, organized, and possibly entertaining lecture and course. Whether or not the students learn is not the instructor's responsibility. The other perspective is that the entire purpose of teaching is student learning (Barr & Tagg, 1995). Student learning is what matters. Just like with writing a book, one needs to reach and connect with the audience. If students are not learning, instructors need to work with them to get them to learn, even if it requires teaching them to learn; or better yet, setting up a structure that encourages them to teach themselves to learn. When questioning our assumptions about what makes education effective, we need to change our focus from good teaching to good learning.

This book is intended as a guide for professors and instructors of all types, especially teaching assistants. In addition, I want to reach those who may teach college students in the future or those who are simply interested in discussing the topic. Further even though the book is a guide for those responsible for instructing, it is not as much about what instructors are doing as it is about what students are doing during the process of being instructed. My vision of the contrarian instructor is one who is less concerned with instruction than with moving their students' learning skills forward.

THE ROLE OF THE CONTRARIAN

Steven Sample published *The Contrarian's Guide to Leadership* when he was President of the University of Southern California. I admire it. As a textbook, it was designed for students taking a class in leadership to question some of the most common tenants of leadership theory. Here are some of Sample's contrarian examples:

- Usually leaders are taught to make fast and dramatic decisions. Quick and direct action makes one appear strong and in control. As a contrarian, Sample suggests the opposite. Leaders should be slow and deliberate. In the long run, it is important to wait to make the most important decisions only when necessary. Sample shows how this can allow more information to become available and to provide time for careful deliberation.
- Conventional leadership wisdom often advocates for delegation and suggests relying on experts when one doesn't understand an issue. As a contrarian, Sample outlines the reasons to be leery of the advice from experts.
- Leaders typically think they must stay informed about the latest news and events, especially those that may possibly have an influence on their enterprise. As a contrarian, Sample claims that there may be advantages of not attending to current events. Often, the latest news is a distraction and the important news is best when conveyed and interpreted by a number of others.
- Niccolò Machiavelli is often vilified for advocating that "the end justifies the means." This aphorism is typically interpreted as any bad

deed is justified if the purpose is pure. Although refraining from supporting the conduct of inappropriate deeds, the contrarian Sample champions good old Niccolò. He is able to show how Machiavelli did have some important insights about human nature in the gray zone where good-and-bad acts intersect with good-and-bad purposes.

Sample uses his contrarian positions to get the reader thinking. As I will review in Chapter Thirteen, there are typically few right or wrong answers concerning approaches to leadership. One may or may not support Sample's positions more than the conventional theories of leadership. But Sample is able to use the contrarian approach to provide a contrast that fosters examination, evaluation, interpretation, and discussion about the pros and cons of different approaches and different behaviors. Taking an extreme, and nontraditional view, is a common device for facilitating examination of the essential points in any argument.

THE CONTRARIAN INSTRUCTOR

I have applied Sample's contrarian approach to thinking about student learning. Specifically, in the following chapters I will stake out several positions that may seem contrary to educational theory or at least to conventional approaches to college teaching. These positions are designed to promote thinking about ways to connect the value system of the instructor to the value system of the student. Here are some contrarian examples:

- Students should learn how to do things, and get experience with practicing any activity, before they are given the theory for why they are doing it or how it works.
- In fact, teaching theory should usually be avoided.
- To promote learning, it is better to teach a class than to take a class. Teaching in the hallways and student-union dining room may be better than teaching a class.
- Covering all of the material planned for a course is not of much value. Facts and information are easy to get when needed. Knowing about something is not as important as wanting to know more about something.

- Redundancy is good. If something is worth saying once, it is worth saying again a little differently.
- A detailed and sequenced curriculum, having a large number of required courses or general education requirements, is often detrimental.
- What students are doing, and learning to do better, is more important than what an instructor is saying. Skill and wisdom don't come in a lecture.
- Students should learn to be confident in their own answers. Being right is not as important as learning to justify ones answers.
- The act of taking an examination is a great learning experience. Students should devote a lot of time to taking examinations. Using examinations to evaluate or motivate students is secondary, it not overrated.
- Even the best scholarship can benefit from some bling.
- Advances in technology have been incredible. In education, they change everything. They just don't matter much in relation to leading students to become more mature and talented learners.
- Learning should be motivating for the students. It may also be work. The reinforcement should come, not from grades or other accolades, but from the benefits of using the skills just learned.
- The instructor is more responsible for the setup of the classroom than the architect or the custodian.
- Instructors should not lay out everything ahead of time. Learning activities, lectures, and even courses benefit greatly if there is a twist at the end. If students discover an unexpected insight near the culmination of the learning experience, it has the potential to make a bigger impact on them; and thus to be remembered and transferred to new situations.

Did you find something, anything, to disagree with on this list? I hope so. If not, you may not wish to continue reading. But, if you do disagree, then read on. I intend to make points that get you thinking. We all should be examining the assumptions embedded in our approaches to cultivating student learning— are we connecting with student values in a way that inspires them to learn on their own, to become mature learners?

Even if one might disagree with any particular position, one may realize there is ample room for thoughtful innovations in our educational approaches.

As we will see in the chapter on critical thinking, asking the right questions takes a skill based on scholarly experience and the best questions do not have easy answers. The purpose of this book is to get instructors to ask powerful and thought-provoking questions about typical assumptions for designing a lecture and a class. Perhaps this will lead to experimentation and possibly changes in the design and implementation of many courses as well as in curricular design.

THE TRADITIONAL INSTRUCTOR

Throughout this book I will be discussing contrarian ideas about student learning. This is in contrast to the traditional approach of many instructors. The following summarizes my impressions of a traditional instructor:

- The traditional instructor knows his or her discipline well and loves it. Instructors have insight into the salient concepts of their subject matter. It is why they were hired and how they can advance in academia. The traditional instructor is strongly motivated to get others to love her or his content area too.
- The traditional instructor believes that the most important part of planning a course is to decide what material to cover and how to pack in as much content as possible.
- The traditional instructor understands that giving good lectures is vitally important. Lectures should be interesting, even entertaining. However, jokes or other flourishes are not necessarily integrated into the concepts the traditional instructor is trying to get across.
- The traditional instructor likes to stop during lectures and ask students if they have any questions. The most common questions are: Can you slow down? Can you repeat that?
- The traditional instructor is likely to give one or two examinations during a semester as well as a final. Examinations are taken by the students during a class period or the designated two-hour slot during finals week. There is a lot of concern about student cheating.
- The traditional instructor often gives students projects to do outside of class and it is not uncommon for students to work in groups in these out-of-class projects. Many such projects concentrate on students exploring information about topics that they select themselves. The

instructor hopes this freedom will allow students to choose content with more interest to them.

- The traditional instructor will lay out everything in an initial outline or syllabus. Surprises, like tricks in a demonstration or stage magic can be embraced as helping to entertain students, but students will be assured that there will be no twists regarding what and how they are to learn.

A fundamental belief of traditional instructors is that their discipline has value in itself. If students are exposed to the insights inherent in the discipline, the students will understand and appreciate its importance. To traditional instructors, teaching is about exposing students to new ideas. Students are responsible for buckling down and learning what is before them. How students might learn or how what they are learning in college is going to make a difference in how they lead their lives is not a direct concern.

THE CONTRARIAN TRADITION

Academics often value[2] the world through the lens of their discipline. This is part of a general aspect of human behavior that psychologists call the *confirmation bias* (Gilovich, 1991; Tavris & Aronson, 2007). The confirmation bias leads all of us to filter and interpret information to affirm and support the salience of our own values and identities. For example, biologists emphasize the centrality of the life of plants and animals on Earth. Geologists know that the rocks and dirt that make up Earth are the foundation for it all. Chemists point out that all plants, animals, and rocks are made of chemicals. Physicists can make a very good case that physics is the infrastructure supporting not just chemistry but all areas of science. In a similar discipline-centric way, linguists have asserted, not just the importance of human communication, but that language is what makes us human. More than bipedal locomotion, facility with tools, or opposable thumbs; linguists claim that the fundamental distinctions separating humans from other animals are the universal characteristics in the form and substance of our many languages.

---

[2] Notice that the term here is "value" not "view."

As an educator, I jump into this discussion with an approach that advocates for the centrality of education. I posit that the human practice of deliberately and systematically helping each other, especially the youth, to sharpen and refine learning skills is the fundamental difference that makes our species special. Further, it is developing the skill to think critically as reviewed in Chapter Five that is the central benefit of our educational practices. In this context, critical thinking is the skill of being able to recognize and articulate all sides of an issue, to evaluate the evidence, and to make rational decisions. This is the heart of education. It is the foundation for literature, mathematics, science, as well as the nonverbal skills inherent in the fine arts. It allows us to shape our world—to create computers, skyscrapers, recombinant DNA, interplanetary probes, world wars, and global warming. This is the gift of being human[3].

Although learning to think critically is the central outcome of education, it can also be turned around and applied to education: Can we be critical about our teaching others to be critical? Humans have been teaching others throughout our history and we have often used critical thinking to evaluate our educational practices. This leads to the contrarian approach. Whenever we teach, we can always look at the purposes for teaching, consider not just traditional practices but contrarian options, and make rational decisions about what is the best approach. Applying the contrarian approach has always been part of education.

As reviewed by Haskins (1923), higher education as we know it had its roots in medieval Europe. The college lecture evolved from preaching. As Haskins reviews the medieval university, it is clear huge differences exist between those traditions and contemporary higher education. Through the centuries we have been trying new pedagogical approaches, making improvements, and championing the effectiveness of traditional practices that we know work well, such as the lecture. One of the greatest innovations in college learning was to combine instruction with research and the emergence of the research university in the last century has been one of our most powerful

---

[3] Oh the hubris of thinking that being human is one-up on the other species. One could claim that our lives are enriched by many aspects that are not specific to humans but are more general attributes of animals. Too often we invoke "human nature" when we really mean to invoke "animal nature." Yes, the human nature aspect of intellect fills and sustains our lives. But, so do to the transspecies values of love, affection, tenderness, devotion, community, competition, and raw sexual desire. Even further, these issues about our place in the world beg one to ask: What makes a life worth living? What gives us meaning? Is there a purpose for why humans are on Earth? Is that different from why other animals are here?

academic accomplishments—both in its benefit to research and to student learning. Even when classes are taught by professors who would rather be in the laboratory, which describes me early in my career, the student experience can be enhanced by the juxtaposition of research and teaching in the same environment. In my earliest days as a professor, I would leave the laboratory at the last minute and run down to the lecture hall which was also on the third floor and wax eloquently, and with passion, about our latest research findings. This is at the heart of the idea of a research university and it has elevated the cultures who foster them to great accomplishments.

Unfortunately, though, the predominance of the research university has a downside. Faculty members can be passionate about their teaching. They love to inspire students. Yet, they love to promote their disciplines and the special insights of their own lines of scholarship even more. A subrosa purpose in many lectures is to get students to think like the lecturer does. Come over to my side. Further, universities, especially research universities, are entrepreneurial environments. Although the public sees universities as socialistic institutions, they are quite capitalistic. Faculty members compete for not just salary increases, but recognition and the resources to make an impact. Scholarship often demands significant resources. The best research ideas are not worth much if one does not have the infrastructure and funding to test them. If the scholarship is not maintained at a cutting-edge level, if it does not do exceptionally well in competitive peer-review with all of the other inspired and productive research, then the resources are lost. Faculty members cannot afford to jeopardize their research. Consequently, although there is interest in improving teaching, the system has not allowed teaching to compete well with the demands of scholarship directly in ones discipline. Yes, innovative teaching has been valued and a great deal of research has helped to evaluate and improve teaching, but the competitive nature of institutions does not allow pedagogical pursuits to match the excitement and enthusiasm that faculty members have for scholarship in their own disciplines. In addition, it has been traditional in some academic units that if a faculty member gets involved in research about teaching in her or his discipline, it is valued less in their yearly peer assessments than if it were research related directly to the discipline.

In universities with a high level of research activity, professors are evaluated predominantly by the quality of their scholarship. I had a first-hand look at how the process operates as I was a provost, associate provost, and department chair. I participated in evaluating the yearly portfolios and promotion decisions of hundreds of faculty members through the years. One begins with the question of whether the individual meets minimum expectations as an effective teacher. The candidates usually do and thus attention turns to evaluation of the scholarship. Quality and quantity of scholarship is what drives most decisions about salary increases, promotion, and tenure. Although, teaching can be intrinsically rewarding for the instructor; with limited resources and temporal capacity, faculty members are driven to spend their innovative efforts on their scholarship. The system provides extrinsic rewards for good teaching, but not enough to allow professors to spend the energy to evaluate the entire process of what teaching is about. Traditionally, there is only the expectation that professors provide clear, organized, comprehensive, and entertaining lectures.

The seminal work of Boyer (1990) began a movement challenging traditional approaches to college instruction. In *Scholarship Reconsidered*, Boyer makes it clear that instructors must take responsibility for student learning. Instructors should be rewarded for innovative teaching, and the scholarship of teaching and learning must be embraced as one of the greatest challenges for every discipline in the contemporary research university. Boyer was a contrarian who was prescient in his understanding of the need to stimulate the scholarship of teaching and learning and powerfully influential in his ability to do so. Much has happened in response to his clarion call. We all must forward the charge.

THREE QUALIFICATIONS

Higher education works very well. In my opinion, and in the opinion of many others, we are doing a superb job in providing valuable college experiences for the vast majority of students. Students do learn. They build on their learning to change their lives and to change the world. The successes of our higher education systems in teaching, scholarship, and service are the envy of the world. They have contributed greatly to the way our country has flourished in the last century and contributed so exceptionally to the world in which we live. These positive qualities of academia have been reviewed by many authors in many ways (see for example, Roth, 2014; Zakaria, 2015).

Still, higher education has been criticized for a variety of reasons; e. g., Arum & Roksa (2010) cite test scores on problem solving; Bennett & Wilezol (2013) consider the costs and raise concerns about vocational focus; Hersh & Merrow (2005) discuss a number of topics such as lowered standards, more focus on ratings than student learning, and faculty members who care too much about research; and Bloom (1987) slams what he sees are inappropriate values. When discussing these popular books criticizing higher education, Derek Bok (2006) summarizes:

> Even the specific practices singled out for criticism such as grade inflation, or political biases within the faculty, or the failure to promote popular lecturers, are seldom ones that have a demonstrable effect on how much students learn or how well equipped they are to live a full and successful life after they graduate (p. 56).

That is an important compass-direction for this book. Our educational system works well. Although colleges are not perfect in many ways, their accomplishments are significant and meaningful. Much of what institutions of higher education do has been remarkably successful. Yet, there is room for improvement. It is our obligation to consider some of the options for improving student learning.

A second qualification is that this book is not meant as a comprehensive or even systematic review of the literature that bears on the points made. There has long been research about good teaching (McKeachie & Svinicki, 2010) and since the call to action by Boyer (1990), the number and scope of studies to improve the efficacy of teaching and student learning have escalated. Other books have compiled and interpreted a great deal of this evidence on the student experience (e.g., Pascarella & Terenzini, 2005). Reviewing the literature in a comprehensive fashion is not the purpose here, further, in many cases, there may not be a lot of evidence for the ideas and suggestions offered. Accordingly, the book intends to motivate instructors to seek more evidence and insight about the student learning that must be directing our teaching efforts. The intent of this book is to be provocative; to present ideas that are controversial or at least not generally accepted. The intent is to stimulate informed discussion, critical thinking, deep learning, and a quest to ask and answer new questions about how teaching guides student learning. Instructors are typically skeptical. It is part of the contrarian nature of a scholar. Hence, for the reader to be skeptical of the ideas in this book is expected and welcomed.

I have employed a somewhat casual writing style. Hopefully it will broaden the readership of this book to those who find most of the work written for a scholarly audience to be obfuscated with a turgid elitist vernacular. As mentioned, the citations are meant to be representative and not as extensive or tied to primary sources as those found in a scholarly monograph. In many cases, I have used the first person pronoun. I have purposely provided personal experiences, anecdotes, and memories. Rather than trying to cite all of the evidence for points made, most of the citations are meant to steer the reader to further reading and other materials. It is difficult to present material in this type of book without appearing authoritarian to the reader. The casual writing style is intended to soften the authoritarian tone. Regardless, this book is intended to be self-reflective. It tries to practice the contrarian style of discovery being advocated; to practice what is preached. Consequently, contrarian-style criticism of the ideas presented is expected and welcomed. Readers should not believe anything written here without analyzing it. Readers should explore ideas introduced here that sound interesting. Then the readers can ask and answer questions of their own.

A third important qualification is that many of the topics of this book, and even the contrarian points made, are not new at all. Similar considerations have been researched and debated through the years by countless curriculum committees, faculty senates, meetings of department faculty members, and centers for faculty teaching excellence. I have benefitted greatly from many such discussions in my roles as professor, administrator, and faculty senate chair. In the last two decades there have been dramatic changes in the way many instructors teach. Some might even consider this to be a revolution spurred by the upsurge in scholarship on teaching and learning. However, although large numbers of instructors are now actively pursuing many of the approaches advocated in this book, many more instructors are teaching in entirely traditional ways. Even in the areas of the most active change, the contrarians are still in the minority.

The intent of this book is to focus on a few recurring ideas, to make some points about them, to provide citations concerning these points to more representative literature where useful, and to offer suggestions for improvement and change. Some of the approaches, like active learning, already have a great deal of momentum. Other contrarian ideas, like significant curriculum change, will be slower to come, if they ever do. For the instructors who will continue to lecture throughout every class and continue with traditional methods, I see no harm in that. The traditional instructors may often do a good job. Perhaps though, if any of the ideas in this book stimulate instructors to try something new, maybe some of their students will move to a deep-learning mode sooner and their development into mature learners will be enhanced. I hope that happens. In the end, the purpose of the book will have been accomplished if it leads to more directed debate and to research testing ideas and options for inspired student learning.

Chapter 2

THE PURPOSE OF A COLLEGE EDUCATION

Motivation is driven by purpose. What is the purpose of getting a college education? Billions of dollars and countless hours are devoted to higher education, what is its purpose? It depends on who you ask. We have a grand tradition, beginning with Aristotle and continuing through John Locke and John Dewey, purporting that education is primarily for the purpose of developing the individual to participate meaningfully in society, to live an informed life, and to further the quest and destiny of humankind. Thomas Jefferson was not only a founding father for our nation, he was also one of the founders of higher education in America. According to Jefferson (1818), the seven purposes of education are:

> To give every citizen the information he (sic) needs for the [1] transaction of his own business; To enable him to [2] calculate for himself, and to [3] express and preserve his ideas, his contracts and accounts in writing; To improve by reading, his [4] morals and faculties; To understand his [5] duties to his neighbors and country, and to discharge with competence the functions confided to him by either; To know his [6] rights… And, in general to observe with intelligence and faithfulness all of the [7] social relations under which he shall be placed" (Cited by the American Academy of Arts and Sciences, 2013, p. 16, numbers in brackets have been added to highlight different purposes).

Jefferson is following Benjamin Franklin's wise council that education is essential for the participation of informed citizens in a democracy (Harkavy &

Hartley, 2008) and, in this case, he itemized even more specific purposes related to leading a richer life[4] Unfortunately, today politicians do not deal with the political need for informed citizens and concentrate on the need for an educated workforce to stimulate economic vitality, often to the extent that they lose sight of the other purposes (Oppong, 2013; Noddings, 2013). That is, political leaders who help states fund both public and private educational institutions, especially governors, see the primary goal of higher education as economic stimulation and workforce development[5].

---

[4] There is a value assumption here that learning is good and that knowledge and insight, science and scholarship, will enhance our lives. The Amish and many luddites have a different world view and they find scholarship, science, and learning in general to be a distraction from what might be most meaningful in life. Eugene Robin (1973) wrote a paper on the evolutionary value of being stupid. His point was that for air-breathing animals living in the sea, having fewer neurons gives them a survival ability of being able to stay under water longer. In the opening scene in the movie, *Animal House*, there is a statue of the founder of Faber College with a quotation underneath: "Knowledge is Good." This was meant to be cute because it was thought that assuming knowledge is good is trivial, not profound. Is it obvious that knowledge, understanding, and intellect are good thing?

[5] Following Jefferson, many lists have been made for the purposes of higher education. Bogue & Aper (2000, p. 34) ask if America's colleges and university are to serve as:

- Instruments of personal and societal improvement?
- Crucibles of dissent and discovery?
- Means for transmitting knowledge and culture?
- Conservators of heritage and knowledge?
- Engines of economic development?
- Curators of humankind's artistic impulses?
- Forums for constructing and evaluating public policy?
- Enemies of injustice, ignorance, and inertia?
- Guardians of human dignity and civility?

Massey (2003) cites his colleague at Stanford, Patricia Bumport, in describing the "social charter of higher education" to:

- Produce an educated citizenry.
- Serve in a compensatory capacity by assisting those who are poor and disadvantaged to have a better life.
- Contribute to economic development by training and retraining workers, and supporting industry's interests with advancements and application of knowledge
- Conduct research for national, state, and local interests.
- Provide a place apart for faculty and students to have academic freedom, to foster cultural critiques and dissent.
- Serve local community settings as a good neighbor or partner
- Provide health care or support through teaching hospitals and medical centers
- Provide entertainment, sports, and high culture.

If one were to ask different faculty members, one might or might not get some of the purposes on Jefferson's list; however, it is very likely that most would extol the joys of 1) becoming a life-long learner, 2) preparation for leading a more fulfilling and informed life, and 3) having the intellectual tools to make this a better world. Bain (2012) explains that: "... learning changes who people are and how they view the world. It makes them into better problem solvers, more creative and compassionate individuals, more responsible and self-confident people" (p. 90). There is good evidence, and many books written, to support the faculty members who extoll the virtues of a liberal science and arts education with the rewards of learning for learning's sake (Kernan, 1999; Colby et al., 2003; Shapiro, 2005; Farrell, 2011; Roth, 2014; and Zakaria, 2015).

Entwistle (1984) has shown that instructors perceive student learning as centering around critical thinking about any subject. Although there may be little data directly on the topic, from Entwistle's conclusion, it is not unreasonable to assume that many faculty members expect students, or at least wish for students, to buy into the primacy of liberal education; i.e., the development of the intellect without regard to whether it is vocational or not (Noddings, 2013).

Here is the disconnect. If one were to ask students their purpose in getting a college education, the students often remark that they want to get a better job than they might get otherwise, one that pays more. Some students might even say that they want a job with more personal rewards and satisfaction. Students might also say that they want the pride and recognition that comes with receiving a degree. As pointed out by Schneider and Humphreys (2005), "students have come to see the college degree as just a ticket to be punched on the way to their first job" (p. B20), and "... liberal education and what it means have slipped off the public radar screen" (B20).

For many decades the most definitive source of information on student attitudes has been the survey conducted by the Cooperative Institutional Research Program at the UCLA Higher Education Institute. They report that 88% of students list getting a better job as their primary reason for attending college. This is a significant increase in that this number was 68% when the

---

The above lists concentrate on the role of the university in society. From the point of view of a student, one should also consider the value of the student-life experience such as purposely leaving home to develop personal independence and responsibility. The joys and obligations of campus life and the college experience add much to the purpose of education for many students (Kuh et al., 1991).

study began asking this question in 1976 (Pryor et al., 2012). In another example, Dana Driscoll (2014) surveyed second- and fourth-semester college students and reported:

> Findings reveal that for many students, vocationalism created a single-minded focus on student's career preparation and major coursework and invites disregard for the value of general education courses that do not appear to immediately relate to students' future careers (abstract).

The students' parents have similar attitudes. Many of them resent the faculty's call for a lifetime of informed learning. For parents, return on investment is critical. College is just too expensive; in time, money, inconvenience, and loss of other opportunities; to support any of Jefferson's other purposes of higher education. Further, in some cases parents may be apprehensive about college challenging their child's commitment to the family's values[6]. A survey done by Daniel Yankelovich (cited by Ferall, 2011) asks prospective students and their parents about why they should attend college. Seventy five percent of the students and eighty-five percent of the parents agreed or strongly agreed with the proposition that college: "Prepares students to get a better job and/or increases their earning potential." Ferrall provides a representative parent comment: "The ultimate goal of college is to get a practical education and secure a first job... Few people believe in the importance of: 'learning for learning's sake' anymore" (p. 50).

The increase in concern for the vocational purposes of college is also reflected in the growth in popularity of majors directly related to entry into a specific profession. Over 100 years ago the great majority of college students majored in the liberal arts and sciences (Ferrall, 2011). Vocational education did not have the status in society of liberal education. That changed dramatically in the first half of the 20th century and continued in the second half. For example, the American Academy of Arts and Sciences (2013) reports that in the past 50 years, the percentage of graduates with a major in the humanities has dropped from 14% to 7%. In contrast, they show significant

---

[6] Children learn from many experiences in many places and circumstances. They learn from their church (or mosque, or synagogue, or temple), their school, and their family. If learning from school is expanded by attending college, there is less emphasis on learning from family and religion and their might even be competing ideas Thus, some parents see education as potentially challenging the lessons about family or religious values they want their children to learn.

increases across many different applied majors and professional degrees. This shift in majors again shows that education is seen, not as a luxury to enrich the mind, but as investment in future vocational prospects. As conceded by Roth (2014): "... pontificating that the best education is nonvocational is really just a trite appeal to the tradition of the leisured gentleman whose status was linked to not having to use his education to earn a living" (p. 160). In today's world, one's profession determines not just economic resources, it also influences ones role and status in society. Education is seen as practical in that it is a route to elevate social status.

What does this have to do with student learning? A number of student beliefs and attitudes will be discussed below, but the most pervasive attitude, and the one that shapes most of their other beliefs and behaviors related to learning in college, is their attitude about why they are in school, the purpose of their education (Harris, 2006). Students want a job, profession, or career that is lucrative, rewarding, and prestigious. They need to realize that it is not the degree, but the learning skills developed in college that are the key to providing a more meaningful life. To quote education writer, Bel Kaufman[7], "Education is not a product, mark, diploma, job, money in that order; it is a process, a never ending process" (Search quotes, 2017).

Yet, society reinforces that grades, awards, and other explicitly identified accolades received in college are what matters. It is easy for instructors to be critical of students for not having an attitude that makes them hungry to learn. However, our students reflect our society. Instructors should strive to understand student motivations and purposes for being in class, rather than being critical of them for not having a scholarly attitude. Students have yet to learn to be scholarly—it is our challenge to get them to want to learn and to learn to learn. Then they will love to learn.

---

[7] Bella Kaufman was advised by her publisher to truncate her name to Bel as there was still discrimination directed at women authors in the 1950s.

Chapter 3

A STUDENT'S PURPOSE DETERMINES A STUDENT'S APPROACH TO LEARNING

In 1976, Marton and Säljö published a seminal study showing that university students can adopt different approaches to learning depending on the purpose they see for their education. The different approaches are surface learning, strategic learning, and deep learning. This pioneering work, published 40 years ago, has spawned a number of studies advocating the grouping of learning approaches (Marton, Hounsell, & Entwistle, 1997). Surface and strategic learning are the most commonly observed behaviors.

As explained by Bain (2012), when in surface learning mode, students concentrate on memorizing facts, figures, and other observations in a form that represents how the information was presented to them. Students try to remember so they can repeat the information when expected by the instructor. They are the students who raise their hands and ask: "Will that be on the test?" As explained by Bain (2012) "... surface learners usually only focus on passing the exam, not on ever using anything they read" (p.36). When in this mode, they do not try to move to higher levels of analysis such as those in Blooms' taxonomy (Krathwohl, 2002) which might include understanding on a level that can explain what they have memorized, applying what they have remembered to new situations, and analyzing and critiquing the assumptions and conclusions inherent in the material. It has long been known that memorizing by itself, putting the information into a mental filing cabinet, doesn't work as well as other learning approaches (Bereiter & Scardamalia, 2005). Long ago, Bartlett (1932) showed that memory works much better if one makes personal interpretations and has a reason for wanting to know and remember something.

The second learning mode is strategic learning. Strategic learning goes beyond memorizing, but it is still entirely directed by what is required by instructors to look good, to get good grades, and to graduate with the highest honors. Strategic learning is working to please others and that is both how and why students in the strategic learning mode prepare for examinations. They study the grading rubric for every assignment and make sure they do what is requested, maybe even more than what was expected. These students are astute observers of the extrinsic reinforcements inherent in our higher education system and they play the game to win those reinforcements. When compared to surface learning, strategic learning strategies work much better for students playing the education game. Students who concentrate on the strategic approach often thrive at school and garner great praise from their instructors, peers, and especially parents.

Students who concentrate on strategic learning are serious about their life goals, especially the vocational ones, and they wish to get ahead in life. Unfortunately, they are not pursuing the best methods for doing so. They are not asking their own questions about the material. They are not challenging the veridicality of what they are told or what they read, nor are they considering its utility. When in this mode, students pay little attention to whether or not the content of the material is meaningful to them. They do not see their purpose for being in the class, or as explained above, for being in higher education, as learning material that might influence what they believe, how they act, or what they feel (Bain, 2012).

The third learning strategy reviewed by Marton, Hounsell, & Entwistle (1997) is deep learning. When practicing deep learning, students are driven by their own questions and their own desire to understand more about them. Thus, deep learning directly reflects the idea of liberal education for the sake of learning to learn well. When deep learning is occurring, students have questions, which are their own questions, about life and the world. Those questions drive their curiosity. They look at their college experience as an opportunity to answer some of those questions and to develop the tools to continue to seek answers throughout their lives. Unlike surface learning where one is trying to fill a mental filing cabinet, deep learning involves answering one's own questions and thus one develops a framework to facilitate remembering (Alfieri et al, 2011). Students practicing deep learning are motivated to understand the meaning behind every lecture and every text. They think about implications. They critically analyze arguments and consider applications. They learn how to create their own arguments and their own solutions. They are using all of the levels of Bloom's taxonomy, especially the highest levels related to creativity. Such students are crafting the tools to be able to learn more, to learn independently, to learn with intent, and to learn to make a difference. They are reflecting the scholarly values of their faculty mentors as they pursue the primary purpose of liberal education—developing more powerful learning skills.

Ambrose et al. (2012) discussed the concept of *far transfer*. Transfer is the application of skills, knowledge, or approaches that are learned in one place to a different application or a new context. Transfer is said to be *near* if there is a lot of similarity between the learned and applied context, or if the application happens quickly after initial learning. An example of near transfer is when one learns a concept and then moves directly into doing a task that employs the concept. Transfer is said to be *far* when the contexts are quite different. An example might be learning a skill in one class and using it in another class. Ambrose et al. (2012) assert that: "Far transfer is, arguably, the central goal of education: we want our students to be able to apply what they learn beyond the classroom" (p.108). Although I would assert that the central goal of education is to learn to be good at learning, I would agree with Ambrose et al. that far transfer is a necessary component of learning. Driscoll (2014) states: "How well students are able to transfer knowledge beyond general education courses is imperative to upholding the principles and long-term viability of higher education" (p. 21).

Ambrose et al. show that the further the transfer, the more difficult it is for students. Far transfer is especially challenging for surface and strategic learners; this is because people are more likely to remember something if it matters to them (Ambrose et al., 2012). How many of us have had students in one class not remember basic insights and understanding from a prerequisite class in the preceding semester? That is a failure of far transfer (Lang, 2013). Following the analogy to the mental filing cabinet, Bereiter & Scardamalia (2005) explain that we cannot just file facts. We don't remember well unless we have a framework to support the ideas to remember. Deep learning involves finding answers to one's own questions and doing so provides the framework. Deep learning facilitates far transfer and that is a fundamental outcome of education.

Some authors, like Bain (2012), talk about categorizing students as being either surface learners, strategic learners, or deep learners. Yet, Marton, Hounsell, & Entwistle (1997) explain that learning styles are typically situational. That is, a student who approaches most challenges as a strategic learner may switch to deep learning if he or she sees the purpose for learning about a topic and has questions for which she or he would like answers. We all tend to be curious about our own interests, hobbies, and ideas about what we need to know to inform our lives in the future. Such curiosity tends to move us into deep-learning mode[8].

Many students begin college focused on surface or strategic learning. Their objective is to get a rewarding job after graduation. Yet, they can evolve as they get closer to finishing their degree. They begin to worry about learning to do the job for which they are preparing. They begin to want to know how to practice in their future profession. In many cases, this can lead the student to asking questions and deep learning, yet in my opinion, it doesn't happen enough. Many students have not been prepared to ask probing questions and to search for answers on their own. They want the instructor and the textbook to give concrete answers that provide detailed, specific formulae for professional practice. As surface or strategic learners, they want the recipe they can follow that explains how to do their future jobs. They are not yet thinking about getting the background to make informed discretionary decisions as practitioners of their future professions. The students usually don't consider that they may change jobs and professions during their careers and that they need learning skills that can be transferred from one challenge to another. Instructors cannot blame students for this mindset, it is a product of our society. This is more related to higher education's failure to understand the student attitude at the start of their college education than anything the student has done.

A few years ago I was discussing student learning approaches with a faculty colleague. He insisted that students could do both strategic and deep learning. He asserted that if we design the learning experiences well enough, then even though students would be driven as strategic learners to answer questions we had posed rather than their own questions, the process of doing what they were asked to do and thinking what they are asked to think could lead them to their own questions and feed their own curiosity. This colleague was asserting that strategic learning leads to deep learning. I am sure this happens, but I would propose that it does not happen often enough. That is because our educational system overemphasizes extrinsic rewards and those incentives crowd out the deep learning. Let me explain.

---

[8] However, be careful. Although our personal interests can move us into deep learning mode, it is not important for instructors to pick content that matches a student's prior interests. If material is clear and there are challenges that are manageable, the thrill of solving the puzzles and viewing new vistas can move students into deep learning even in areas with no prior interest.

As explained in the classic book on teaching excellence (McKeachie & Svinicki, 2006) and like so many things in life, education is filled with both extrinsic and intrinsic rewards. Extrinsic rewards are artificial, but they are meant to motivate work and to recognize accomplishments. Extrinsic rewards are merit badges. They are test scores. They are grades. They are diplomas. In contrast, intrinsic rewards are not very tangible but they are inherent in being able to do what is learned. Intrinsic rewards are the primary reason for taking on the learning activity. For example, the extrinsic reward for practicing the piano as a child might be a gold star. The intrinsic reward might be the joy in being able to play a song on the piano. Extrinsic rewards are public, at least at first. Then later, like a child's gold star, they are forgotten. Intrinsic rewards are not very obvious in the nascent stages of learning. That changes. When one learns a skill, even a skill like becoming a good learner, the rewards are much more obvious when one becomes adroit. When the talent is significant, the rewards come from the joy of using the talent. Extrinsic rewards then become secondary, if not dismissed as a vestige of the past.

Surface and strategic learning are driven by extrinsic rewards. Deep learning is driven by the intrinsic rewards of being able to understand and to do something as a skilled practitioner. Ryan & Deci (2000) have shown that extrinsic rewards can take the focus away from deep learning. Yet, I would agree with McKeachie & Svinicki (2006) and Pintrich & Garcia (1991) that both extrinsic and intrinsic rewards are useful in many educational pursuits. A kind word, a pat on the back, an appreciative smile, or a compliment are all extrinsic rewards and they are great to receive. In many contexts extrinsic rewards are a useful tool for shaping behavior and moving one to a longer-range goal of being able to benefit from the intrinsic rewards. But one needs to be careful. It is easy for all of us to over-interpret the extrinsic rewards, to neglect that the extrinsic rewards are artificial, and to confuse the purpose of an activity as pursuing an extrinsic reward and forgetting about the real purpose, the intrinsic rewards. It is incumbent on us, as instructors, to be explicit in our recognition of the importance of the intrinsic rewards of learning for the sake of learning. We should be constantly asking how we can build more intrinsic motivation into our classes that will foster more deep learning.

Psychologists have grouped information a person would get about his or her performance on any task into two types: summative feedback and formative feedback. Shute (2008) reviews good practices in generating feedback and explains the following. Summative feedback documents what one has done and it is public. Others can see and recognize what was accomplished. It brands the output as a job well done or not so well done. Formative feedback is more private. It is the personal feedback that helps one refine performance and to form new behaviors. Because it is private, formative feedback can be used to ask the hard questions, the probing questions, the questions about areas in need of improvement. The problem is that if the formative feedback becomes public, then it is recognized by others as summative feedback. We all want to look good to others. We want to put our best-foot forward. Consequently, if the formative feedback becomes public then we quit asking the hard questions. Even though the hard questions are the ones that may help us to improve, we tend to sacrifice potential improvement for looking good publicly. Thus, summative feedback swamps formative feedback if one tries to do both at the same time. It is the same for extrinsic and intrinsic rewards in education. Too much emphasis on extrinsic rewards will gloss over the intrinsic rewards. Instructors and students will lose sight of the larger purposes of higher education. We need to remind ourselves that in the long run students are not there to learn about this topic or that discipline. Students are not there to get a degree. Students are not there to get a ticket for a better job. Students are there to learn to learn and to learn to inform their lives.

The prolegomena of this book includes a summary of a graduation speech given by a high-school valedictorian, Erica Goldson. The following is a quote of the opening lines from that same graduation speech (Goldson, 2010):

> There is a story of a young, but earnest Zen student who approached his teacher, and asked the Master, "If I work very hard and diligently, how long will it take for me to find Zen?" The Master thought about this, then replied, "Ten years." The student then said, "But what if I work very, very hard and really apply myself to learn fast - How long then?" Replied the Master, "Well, twenty years." "But, if I *really, really* work at it, how long then?" asked the student. "Thirty years," replied the Master. "But, I do not understand," said the disappointed student. "At each time that I say I will work harder, you say it will take me longer. Why do you say that?" Replied the Master, "When you have one eye on the goal, you only have one eye on the path."

Chapter 4

THE REFLECTIVE-PRACTICE APPROACH
TO DEEP LEARNING

Lee Shulman (2005) developed the idea of a *signature pedagogy* for the curriculum of each discipline or profession. The concept is that each discipline has a signature pedagogy reflecting the "types of teaching that organize the fundamental ways in which future practitioners are educated for their new professions" (p.52). For example, as explained by Brackenbury, Folkins, & Ginsberg (2014) the curriculum is different for law school students than medical school students. Traditionally in law school, the students analyze appellate court cases through Socratic dialog in an auditorium setting in a manner that develops their ability to think in the abstract and to approach cases with the mind-set of a lawyer. Relatively less emphasis is placed on the pragmatic activities of practicing law, such as personal experience dealing with clients. In medical school, more emphasis is placed on the practical decisions that physicians make in diagnosis and treatment through direct contact with patients at the bedside and in grand-rounds experiences. Both medicine and law include theoretical and practical content, but there are differences in their place and form in the curriculum. These differences reflect the signature pedagogies of the two disciplines. Further, the distinctive elements of the signature pedagogy in any discipline are prevalent in most, if not all, programs in that discipline across the country. Shulman (2005) explains that signature pedagogies can and do evolve over time as the needs and values of any profession evolve.

Schön (1983, 1987) also wrote about curricular distinctions across disciplines and, although he forwarded his ideas well before Shulman (2005) did, many of his positions comport with those of Shulman. Schön categorized curricular design as following into one of two general approaches. The first approach is *theory-first practice*. As suggested by the name, theory-first practice will introduce students to theory and foundational information early in the curriculum and slowly move from a diet of all theory to more practical topics related to professional practice. The curricula of undergraduate majors in the physical sciences are examples of theory-first practice. A steady sequence of theoretical classes begins with broad topics and focuses later on theories in more specific areas. Although there may be laboratory sessions that go with these courses, the laboratory activities deal with only a small portion of the functional activities of practicing as a scientist. One must go to graduate school to be exposed to many aspects of day-to-day practice in these fields. Perhaps most importantly, the undergraduate curriculum, and especially afternoon laboratory sessions in the sciences, offer very little exposure to unsolved problems. In these laboratory exercises, students follow directions and manipulate equipment to get a correct answer; that is, an answer that is predetermined. Doing something as prescribed by the instructor is strategic learning. Yet, scientists are motivated primarily by the thrill of asking questions about our world and seeking insight into questions about the unsolved problems, the unknown (Firestein, 2012). As Firestein explains, undergraduates do not get the thrill of developing their own questions, they get the answers that scientists have developed already. Students are not witness to the curiosity that drives the researcher. The theory-first curriculum does not motivate students to move from surface or strategic learning to deep learning.

Many students are turned off by their undergraduate experiences in the physical sciences. This happens even though the science curriculum has much going for it: 1) content that is intriguing and powerful in its implications, 2) significant relevance to our daily lives, 3) great potential for future developments; 4) and, of most importance to students given their strategic attitude, lucrative and prestigious vocational options. In spite of these motivators, it is often only a few students who develop the desire to learn more science on their own because undergraduate courses have piqued the curiosity and the drive for deep learning. The theory-first approach is not good at moving students from surface or strategic learning to deep learning.

Schön explains that theory-first curriculum can work well as preparation for job placements that are concrete and rigorously structured. These are jobs in which there are right or wrong answers, consistency, logical processes, and little ambiguity. These are jobs with little discretion or room for creativity. Most of the more intellectually and creatively demanding professions requiring a college education, including those in the physical sciences

(Firestein, 2012), are not like this. Schön (1987) notes that the most interesting questions a practitioner may wish to ask are the messy ones that will not be obvious in either how to form the question or how to interpret the ambiguities in the findings.

Schön's (1983, 1987) alternative pedagogical approach is *reflective practice*. In reflective practice students receive practical experience in the earliest stages, including hands-on activities and personal experience making decisions. In contrast, theory-first practice concentrates on learning *about* something before learning how to do it or really caring about it. Reflective practice is learning *how* to do the activity and this then motivates deep learning about it. In reflective practice, theoretical perspectives come at a point when students begin to ask questions and benefit from the theory to help answer their own questions about how to practice.

Imagine a student is learning to become an accountant. If the curriculum begins with a survey of theory, the history of those theories, and a comparisons of competing theories; the student is likely to go into strategic learning mode. The student may not be compelled to understand the theoretical material for its intrinsic rewards. In contrast, imagine that a student is confronted with a challenge related to; for example, long-term projections of a company's profit based on different assumptions about how alternative decisions may affect the outcome. How might the reflectice student proceed? A good approach is to search for how others have done it. Then to find patterns in what has been most successful, and finally the student will realize that the successful approaches are organized by underlying theories. Then the student is ready and anxious to learn the theory. Students move into deep learning mode as they have problems to solve and want to learn to solve them.

The name, reflective practice, emphasizes that students are reflecting on their own work and attempting to be productive. Because of this, students are not only driven to understand theory for their own purposes as a deep learner would, but they also become better at far transfer. They see how useful the theory is to further their own goals. They learn theory not because they are told about it, but because they have developed their own questions that need answers. Hence, they remember what they have learned. This is the antidote to the far transfer problem mentioned in the previous chapter. Unlike the theory-first approach, reflective practice is most appropriate for educating practitioners in fields that require discretion and difficult judgments that may be complex, unique, vague, and variable. These are fields in which judgments must be made among competing ideas, demands, and values. These are the professional fields where the practitioners benefit most from a liberal education (Mann, Gordon, & McLeod, 2009).

Schön's (1983) work is over 30 years old. Is there any evidence that it works? Wenger (1998) shows that reflective practice can lead to the social practices of cooperating and sharing of ideas. Marton & Booth (1997) stress the importance of making the deep learning approach explicit for students. Mann, Gordon, & McLeod (2009) have done an historical review of the literature on reflective learning strategies and they found many studies across different disciplines demonstrating how reflective practice fosters deep learning and critical thinking; for example, see Boud & Walker (1998), Glaze (2001), Hattery (2003), Hertzog & Wlliams (2007), and Moon (2005).

An example of reflective practice is how music performance is generally taught. At the youngest ages students begin with an instrument. They are given little theory, but a lot of advice on how to manipulate the instrument and how to play the music. This is followed by great amounts of unsupervised practice, punctuated by frequent meetings to perform for an instructor. They do get extrinsic rewards, like gold stars. They have occasional recitals where the expectations are tailored to their level of ability. The recitals give experience in performing like a practitioner and provide intrinsic rewards and motivation. Music theory comes slowly at the times when the developing musicians may need it to mature and develop their individual styles and abilities. Although students learn to play at an early age, formal courses in music theory are not encountered typically until the undergraduate curriculum. Even then, students are encouraged to be creative in how they interpret and apply music theory. Students are most responsible, not for reciting music theory, but for how they can use it. Just as a deep learner would be.

The historical model of a master craftsman and an apprentice is both a further illustration of the operation of the reflective practice model and an indication that this approach to learning may have a long record of success. The master gives the apprentice a basic task and tells him or her exactly how to do it. The apprentice follows the directions explicitly and builds a body of work. There is extrinsic reinforcement for this accomplishment: "Look what I've made!" More importantly, there is intrinsic reinforcement as the apprentice can use the skills just developed to approach the next project. The apprentice is given harder tasks and in the process complications or unforeseen factors influence the creative activity. The apprentice reflects on the problems and asks questions of the master. These are questions that matter to the apprentice. In the process, the master explains the useful aspects of the theory or the apprentice just figures it out on his or her own. Over time, the performance expectations are increased. The apprentice asks more questions and solves more problems. The success provides more intrinsic reinforcement. The theoretical understanding is increased as the apprentice reflects how important the theory is to informing performance. She or he is functioning as a deep learner[9].

The concept of teaching as reflective practice may go back further still; one might even wonder if we are innately wired for reflective-practice learning. For example, when toddlers learn to talk they are doing their own reflective practice. There are even spurts when young children will learn up to seven words a day and remember them for use throughout their lives. Language learning can involve instruction[10], but much of it is learned spontaneously through reflective practice. One can also think about our prehistoric ancestors as hunter-gatherers. How did they teach their children? I don't expect we have much evidence about that, but one can imagine that a parent might take a child out onto the savannah and the two of them would hunt together. The child would get direction and instruction during the practice of hunting. The child would need to make decisions and would ask questions to improve those choices. The child would learn how to *do* the skill. There would not be theory-first lectures. However, having said that, there might have been many stories told in the evening over the campfire about hunting. The stories bolster the thrill and values of a hunting culture and indirectly give direction on the theory of hunting. The child is then learning *about* the skill. Lecture has its place, but at its best it supplements and stimulates a desire to know how to do something that is imbedded in learning through practice[11].

Here is another example of the reflective practice approach in comparison to traditional methods. Imagine that there was a new software system to use at work; such as a new learning management system or financial package. Everyone needs to learn to use it. In the traditional approach, all employees potentially using the package would be required to come to a seminar that would be done either in-person or online. The instructor would be enthusiastic and cheerful. She would spend a few minutes explaining why the new package

---

[9] This may be an apocryphal description of the master-apprentice relationship. One might also envision a situation in the authoritarian structure of many cultures in previous centuries in which the master craftsman would provide overly specific and rigid orders and the apprentice was given very little opportunity to experiment and to learn.

[10] Speech-language pathologists often use structured exercises to greatly benefit children with delayed language development.

[11] This example, is from Clark Aldrich (2009), *Complete Guide to Simulation and Serious Games*, Introduction: The Campfire and the Veld.

is necessary and how big an improvement it will be. The new system will be worth the effort and cost of everyone taking the time to learn it. If you already knew this and agreed, then you would be eager to learn. But often, you do not care as the decision has been made and you just need to endure the chore of learning the new system. The instructor of the computer seminar then goes on to an explanation of the basic components and processes of the new system. There is a long section on the theory of how all of the different processes fit together for maximum efficiency and power. It is theory first. There might be a number of examples with specific procedures to do: fill this box, scroll down, click here, choose this from menu B, et cetera. The instructor asks questions like: Does everyone understand? Am I going too quickly? If you have questions, they are like: Could you repeat that? Your job is to take notes and worry on your way back to the office if you will be able to remember the long string of commands to make anything work. It can be frustrating when you do sit down and use the program on your own. With some trial and error, you do learn it, maybe with a few calls to the helpline.

Compare this to a more reflective practice. You have a discussion with an instructor about what is dysfunctional or awkward with the existing computer system. The instructor addresses these issues and invites you to watch a skilled user of the new package. First the skilled user does a task. Then she or he slows down and explains each step to you. You ask questions like: Why did you do that? Show me again how you did that? How will this address my concerns about functionality? Then you take turns with the skilled user in carrying out steps. This is followed by you doing a few of the processes under supervision, first close, and then more intermittently. Then you are left to use the program on your own with the confidence, understanding, and an expectation that you will like using it well enough to spend time exploring new applications and processes from the ones you learned first. At this point, you are developing an interest in the theory involved in its most effective use. As you are in deep learning mode, you develop the tools to do this on your own. Wouldn't you agree that the reflective practice approach is more appealing and will result in more and better insight, understanding, and future opportunities?

This example of the software system doesn't have to be only with one-on-one tutoring. Imagine a situation in which a group of students watches the instructor doing the practice in the initial stages. Note, they are not listening to the theory, just watching the practice. Then slowly each student works on a computer to perform tasks at the initial stages. It may even be that the instructor does most of the work, but occasionally asks the students to fill in something. Students are organized in groups so they can ask each other when they have questions. In the next stage, the students are slowly doing some of their own problems, continuing to ask each other for advice, and the instructor is circulating in the room. Students are given assignments to redo the last project on their own computers. Students are reflecting on what they are doing.

The system is encouraging the students to ask questions, questions that are their own. They have a puzzle. They are motivated to solve it. They reflect, explore, and learn. When they seek answers and find them they remember them. Reflective practice is the heart of learning. Reflecting on the practice of reflective practice is the central activity of a contrarian instructor.

Chapter 5

CRITICAL THINKING TO FOSTER REFLECTIVE PRACTICE AND DEEP LEARNING

One of the fundamental themes of this book is: How do we move students' surface or strategic learning behaviors to more deep learning? Schön (1983) would stress that this should be done through reflective practice. For Schön, education is not what students learn to know, but what students learn to do; and most importantly, how they can learn to do it better. How do we create learning environments to facilitate reflective practice? A number of topics will be considered in later chapters to address this issue. However, a theme that underlies these later chapters is that students need to learn to use the processes of scholarly inquiry. Although often misunderstood by the public, the academic tern for such scholarly inquiry is *critical thinking*. Many people look at scholarship as knowing specific information about detailed, and somewhat obscure, areas of research. The contrarian would point out that one can look up information. Rather than being able to retrieve esoterica, critical thinking and the processes involved in making reasoned judgments form the bedrock of scholarship. Beyond scholarly pursuits, critical thinking is the foundation for being able to lead the rest of our lives with purpose. Although we typically do not put it in such a crude way, critical thinking is being principled about deciding who and what to believe and who and what to be.

The term, critical thinking, begs the question: What thinking is not critical? Functioning as a surface learner might not be critical, but memorization and regurgitation does take some thinking. Critical thinking, in the sense used here, is about pursuing a scholarly approach to analyzing any issue. Yet, it is not just for scholars to use or to reserve for those moments when we might delve into some erudite colloquy. When considering learning in general, students learn much more in their lives before they go to college than when they go to college. Graduates learn much more about life after they go to college than they did while in college. The unique aspect of the college experience is not that students learn a lot, but that they get better at applying critical thinking skills in a substantive and meaningful way. This enhances their ability to learn. A central thesis of this book is that college is not about being exposed to, and remembering, content. Another thesis is that college is not very much about learning skills that prepare students for specific professions. College is fundamentally about honing and expanding a student's facility as a critical thinker. College is what makes graduates more powerful learners through the rest of their lives. Although, much of our curriculum does not directly reflect this general idea, I find that faculty members generally do agree with it. Indeed, DeAngelo et al. (2009) found that 99% of faculty members endorse teaching critical thinking as an important goal in a college education. We need to ensure that a primary goal of our collegiate instruction is to guide students to advance their critical thinking skills (Finn, Brundage, & DiLallo, 2016; Folkins, 2016).

A fundamental point of this book is that knowing who to believe, and the constructs one can use to figure out what to believe, is central to being educated. As we live our lives, we are constantly receiving advice on what to think and what to do. Written texts, the media, documentaries, lectures, and communication of all sorts are filled with others giving advice or direction. Some advice is embedded in revered writings; i.e., canonical texts such as Plato's *Republic*, the plays of Shakespeare, Adam Smith's *The Wealth of Nations*, or Charles Darwin's *Origin of Species*. Some is from authorities who have wisdom in a discipline that we don't have; i.e., textbooks, trade books, or how-to manuals written by skilled and respected practitioners. Yet, much of the advice comes from a P.T. Barnum-like character trying to sell us something. The bigger the exaggeration in what the producers are trying to sell us, the greater potential gain for themselves. The point is that we all know that much of what we see, hear, and read about how the world works, or should work, must be interpreted with caution. Scholarship is knowing how to evaluate and assess the various sources of input related to facts, opinions, and directives; making meaning from them, and charting a considered, substantive, and valued path.

One can argue that any healthy teenager has already developed facility at being a skeptic. Teenagers are the "progeny of Bart Simpson" (Edmundson,

1997, p. 10). Instructors do not teach students to be skeptical, being skeptical is endemic in our society. Yet, it takes well-directed reflective practice for college students to learn to marshal their skeptical skill into creative thinking as defined here.

Ideas about critical thinking go back at least as far as Socrates, if not further. A principle component of the Socratic method is to ask the right questions about the logic pertaining to any point one is making. Critical thinking was also championed in the classic works by John Dewey over 100 years ago (Dewey, 1910) although he referred to it as *reflective thinking*[12]. In the late 1960s and 1970s there was a significant upsurge in the idea of teaching critical thinking in the college curriculum, not just as implicit in the presentation of scholarly content, but as a process that students could recognize and learn explicitly. Thus allowing application to any content, scholarly or not, encountered in the future. Students would learn to think about their own thinking—a concept that psychologists commonly call metacognition. Many universities developed courses designed explicitly to teach students critical thinking and scores of textbooks have been written to support these courses. Through the years the popularity of critical thinking courses, usually designed for students in the first year or two of college, have waxed and waned. There appears to be an upsurge of interest in critical thinking courses at present. Stand-alone courses on critical thinking are now common. In addition, it was noted above that many instructors recognize the importance of critical thinking. It is encouraging that many of the stand-alone courses on critical thinking are supplemented by instructors who are explicit about the processes of critical thinking as embedded in discipline-based subject matter encountered later in the curriculum (Finn, 2014).

What specifically is critical thinking? What are the basic processes to be mastered by the reflective practitioner of critical thinking? Different scholars have used a variety of terms and have described the processes of critical thinking somewhat differently. When used in a scholarly context, encomia are directed to critical thinking, as witnessed in the preceding paragraphs. Yet, instructors are often not specific about what is being praised and the term,

---

[12] Personally, I prefer Dewey's reflective thinking term to critical thinking. It is too easy to confuse critical thinking with the process of being critical or finding fault. In my usage, critical thinkers are often being constructive, not itemizing reasons to find fault. A. O. Scott (2016) points out that there is an additional usage of critical thinking: the actions of a professional critic evaluating art, music, theater, or film. Such critics do find fault on occasion, but they are most motivated to find the joy in a really moving work. In the arts and elsewhere, critics are primarily promoters.

critical thinking, can be misused. For example, instructors might claim that students come to their classes with many misconceptions about the world; the instructors are able to tell them how the world really works; and as the students now know the answers preferred by the instructors or how the instructors would solve a problem, their thinking is improved. This reflects a misunderstanding about the meaning of critical thinking. Critical thinking is not about knowing the right answers; i.e., being a surface learner. Critical thinking is about the processes of parsing and analyzing an argument in a scholarly way. The rest of this chapter is devoted to explaining the various ways of identifying and describing those processes. College instructors will already know the skill of critical thinking, but they may not have the experience and vocabulary to identify it and help guide their students to learn to improve their critical thinking skills.

A number of different frameworks have been employed to analyze the processes of critical thinking. Each of the dozens of textbooks available has developed its own terms and systems for analyzing and evaluating arguments. Many of these analytical structures work well. One of the more popular frameworks for analyzing critical thinking is employed in the classic textbook by Browne & Keeley (2014), *Asking the Right Questions*. The material provided below generally follows the Browne and Keeley approach: When analyzing an argument, one must consider the issue, the reasons, the evidence, the significant ambiguities, the assumptions, and the logical fallacies in the reasoning. The review below attempts to touch the highlights of the critical-thinking curriculum. It is meant for illustration. It cannot do justice to the insights accrued in a semester-long class devoted to deep learning about critical thinking, let alone a college education, or a lifetime devoted to honing the reflective practice of critical thinking.

THE ISSUE

When considering the issue of any text or argument, one is asking about the author's primary point. What position is the writer taking and what is being advocated? Is a problem being described or is a solution being offered? Many instructors assume that the issue inherent in an argument is obvious, yet I have found that beginning college students often struggle with finding the issue. The difficulty of grasping the major point of an argument can be illustrated by looking at many students' lecture notes. Often, the students can't write down the main points in their notes, because they don't realize what these points are.

Furthermore, there are times when a very specific argument masks a more global, yet important, point that is only provided implicitly in the material analyzed.

If one reads a paper supporting the need for increased oil fracking in the Midwest, it seems clear that the issue, in the sense used here, is to advocate for this method of producing more oil. However, maybe increased fracking is a means to support the larger issue of advocating for more plentiful energy. Alternatively, maybe the purpose is to counter indirectly claims made by others about global warming. Confusion abounds concerning the larger purpose of an author, the issue driving the argument being analyzed, and even some of the reasons. Students need practice and feedback to learn to focus on the primary issue an author is trying to make in an argument. Students can use a number of hints as they develop facility with finding the issue and being able to do so automatically. These hints include knowing to look in likely locations such as the title or the opening sentence. One also has to learn not to be fooled when the primary issue is never stated explicitly but inferred from the structure of the argument presented.

THE REASONS

Reasons are used to support the author's conclusions about the issue. In the example given above, an author might support the need for more fracking by providing reasons like: 1) fracking does not hurt the environment, 2) shale oil is in abundant supply, 3) the threat of earthquakes produced by fracking is over-rated, 4) there is a need to reduce dependence on foreign oil for defense purposes, and 5) my aunt has been fracking for years and she is still healthy. The critical observer will ask: Why should I believe this author? The quality of the reasons supplies the answer. In my experience, it can often be just as difficult for students to find and assess reasons as it is for them to find the issue. Further, they often confuse the reason with the issue.

Sometimes many reasons and subreasons support the issue. One must also consider how well the reasons are connected to the issue. Sometimes the issue and the reasons are clear and reasonable, but accepting the reasons may not logically lead to agreeing with the author's stand on an issue[13]. One can agree

---

[13] There is an apothegm attributed to Mark Twain: "Clothes make the man. Naked people have little to no influence in society." The issue asserts the importance of dressing well and

with the assertions given in a reason, but challenge the extent to which it supports the issue. Again, as with finding the issue, practice and feedback can make a big difference in a student's ability to describe and analyze an argument's reasons and to assess whether or not the reasons are linked to the issue.

THE EVIDENCE

How good is any reason? As stated, it depends on how well the reasons support the issue, but it also depends on the evidence that supports each reason. How good is the quality of the evidence and how well is the evidence connected to the reasons? There are many different types of evidence. Some academic disciplines rely more on one type of evidence than another. Different scholars may vary on the weight they tend to ascribe to certain types of evidence. Perhaps most of all, within any type of evidence, some evidential findings are much more persuasive than others. Thus it is often necessary for students to develop their skills in evaluating the quality of any evidence as well as their preferences for weighting different types of evidence. Only then can they be adroit at using evidence to interpret the veridicality of a reason.

When teaching critical thinking I developed the following listing of general types of evidence. They are given in descending order of quality.

Order	Type of Evidence	Considerations
1.	Results from research	Especially involving statistics, are the gold standard. Yet, they can be abused by clever writers. The statistics are only as good as the design of the research. Too often the statistics are given without describing the research study. Research is expensive and time consuming. This category includes research findings from scholarship in the humanities.
2.	Analogies	Includes simile, metaphor, and allegory. They can be very insightful in showing complex relationships. Scientists often use them. Some analogies are weak. Avoid begging the analogy.

looking distinctive, which may or may not reflect character. Yet the reason given, concerning the paucity of social influence by nudists, doesn't connect to the issue.

Order	Type of Evidence	Considerations
3.	Appeals to authorities or experts	Often useful and necessary, as well as being practical, especially in specialized fields of knowledge. It's best to know about your expert and avoid *questionable authority*. There are often many levels of authority.
4.	Formal Case studies	Structured reports can be insightful, but avoid generalizing from a small sample just as one must with other types of singular examples.
5.	Lived experiences	Personal observation and memory can be deceiving, as well as concern for generalizing from small samples of behavior. We are biased toward our own interests which is the *conformation bias* described in other chapters.
6.	Witness, personal observations of others	Not as good as lived experiences as you didn't live the situation, you just noticed it.
7.	Testimonials, personal observations from others	Relying on other's observations is not as good as relying on your own. Do you know the value preferences of the person testifying? Are they subject to confirmation bias? When something is retold the confirming evidence is sharpened and other factors are leveled.
8.	Intuition	Better than superstition, but not much. Intuition is more likely to be useful if the person has had a lot of experience in similar situations.

Typically, when one thinks of scholarly evidence the emphasis is on results of research studies and on primary sources for scholars in the humanities. We wish to be rigorous and only except the best evidence. Research can be expensive and time consuming. The better the research, such as in large-sample double-blind clinical trials, the more one can expect high costs and long waits. It is reasonable to reserve getting such expensive evidence for life and death decisions or major scientific initiatives.

The contrarian will caution that the judgment and interpretation of the evidence may be just as important as the evidence itself. Even the best, most resource and time consuming, evidence can be misrepresented. The facts are no better than the theory used to motivate the experiment and the assumptions that went into the design of the study. Alternatively, sometimes scientific experiments that are much less expensive than advanced clinical trials can provide valuable insights into our world. If other experiments take a substantively different approach to insights about the same theory, then their findings can provide especially strong evidence in support of the original idea. Students need to learn to assess the quality of scientific results.

The above discussion is based on experimental evidence in the sciences. In the humanities the evidence comes from many different sources and scholarly paradigms. For example, historians go to original artifacts left by the figures who made or witnessed the historical events they are studying. This evidence is vital to scholarship, it is just gathered with different approaches and assumptions than found in the sciences.

Students in a critical thinking class often assert that they only believe in facts. The question becomes, what is a fact? Although one might think of facts, and the concept of what a fact is, as obvious, Poovey (1998) reviews the history of how the concept of the fact has developed and the assumptions inherent in how scholars now use the concept. On one level, facts are the obvious things that we observe in our world. This was the approach of Aristotle and many philosophers to follow, such as Roger Bacon. The idea is that facts can be plucked as nuggets of experience detached from theory. Today, most scholars do not see such nuggets as valid units of knowledge without identifying some framework, theory, or assumptions used in the construction of the facts. Facts are not theory free nor are they value free. Facts are the results of scholarly inquiry, not the raw inputs. In the sciences, the facts are the findings, that is the data points, from an experiment. Research findings may be as good as it gets to knowing something, at least without invoking assumptions from philosophy or religion. Again, the facts emerging from an experiment are no better than the rigor of the experiment, including the assumptions that went into its design.

Even though there is always a framework in which one must interpret scholarly evidence, for much of what we know and what informs many of the decisions we make, we do not use experimental evidence. People would agree that the city of Paris is in France. It is pretty much indisputable, even for those who have never been to Paris. The point is that we are not doing experiments to demonstrate that Paris is in France. It is just too obvious[14]. We are back to Aristotle's concept that the facts are the kernel concepts about our world that

---

[14] Maybe self-evident is a better term than obvious. The Declaration of Independence contains the famous sentence: "We hold these truths to be self-evident...."

observers generally agree on without need to resort to theory or definitions[15]. This is the rub for the critical thinker. What is so obvious we do not need to challenge it with our critical thinking skills and what is not? Where do we draw the line? What values about a theoretical framework are we willing to accept when assessing data purporting to be facts? What assumptions are we willing to make about whether observations are accurate? Not only are there a number of influences on the evidence we use, often there is no good empirical evidence on which to base a decision. Other times the evidence may be available, but it is not worth the time and effort to get it.

As the table above shows we typically function on the basis of many different types of evidence. It is not possible, or at least practical, to do otherwise. Sometimes it would be better to use an expert's assessment of the evidence than our own. Experts know more about assessing the assumptions used in generating the data and interpreting them within the theoretical framework used to gather the evidence. If a physician tells me I do or do not have a disease, do I believe her? What other expert opinion do I get? How good is that evidence? It is a project in critical thinking.

One of the contrarian themes in critical thinking is that we need expert opinion, yet we need to be careful. I will be considering the legacy of Benjamin Franklin in the next chapter, yet I have not gone to the same evidence that historians would use, the written artifacts left by, or about, Franklin. Instead, I have relied on a book written by an historian (Isaacson, 2003), who interpreted the primary sources and created a secondary manuscript that is more accessible to me. As mentioned above, historians must go to primary sources as the basis and inspiration for their scholarly writing, but the rest of us can use their work as secondary interpretations almost all of the time. For the most part, it would be impractical for nonhistorians to be combing through historical artifacts. Even if nonhistorians were to look at the evidence, they might not have the skills to interpret it well. A similar situation exists in science. Scientists read and refer to the works of other scientists that are published in peer-reviewed scholarly journals. As scientists, we evaluate and interpret the evidence. This is limited to our own areas of expertise. The

---

[15] Interestingly, the Scottish philosopher, David Hume, makes a distinction between synthetic truths that describe matters of fact or self-evident observation (for example, New York has a larger population than Rhode Island) and analytic truths that are true either because of definition or reason (for example, there are twelve inches in a foot, or all mothers are women). Hume would only consider the former to be evidence. The latter would be theory, as least in the way I am using the concepts. See Gottlieb (2016, p. 214) for a more informed philosophical discussion of Hume's insights.

rest of us do not have the tools to do such analysis. In most areas, we don't look at the research evidence; we let other scientists, physicians, journalists, stock brokers, and assorted professionals interpret it for us. A point for the contrarian is that most of the issues we will address through our lives will have reasons that are not based on personal analysis of evidence from research—we rely on others. We need to be skillful, critically thinking, and thus judicious in deciding who to believe. What skills do these experts have and how have they employed them in a way that helps us understand? Some good advice on how to identify which people have expertise and which don't is provided by Hertz (2010) and Levitin (2016)[16].

We have all seen commercials in which some movie star or sports celebrity is endorsing a product. What do these stars know about the product? Is it reasonable for the critical thinker to assume that if this person of respect likes a product, it must be good or that we should buy it? Maybe they do use it or know something about it, but we also know that they are being paid as a spokesperson. They are not necessarily objective. As explained below, it is a logical fallacy to put too much faith in *questionable authority*. Unfortunately, though, following the advice of a questionable authority is endemic in our society. Advertisers know this. The issue is larger than just being enamored by the endorsements of famous people. What about the views of some acquaintance we know and respect? If they like something, it can influence us even if we don't know or agree with their initial reasons for liking it. How about the persons in positions of authority in our lives: parents, teachers including college instructors, employers, wealthy people, politicians, journalists, or religious leaders? They often tell us what to think. In many cases, they are supposed to do so. To some extent we can't help but to be influenced and usually we should be. Yet, we must realize that the persons we respect and wish to follow may be guiding their choices on reasons and evidence with which we would personally not agree. This concern is even more of an issue when many of the people around us have strongly held belief systems. It is just too easy to follow the crowd without taking the time and effort to use ones own critical thinking skills. This is the *ad populum* fallacy.

Some readers might look at the list of types of evidence above and note that analogies are near the top. As deep learners, you are asking yourself, why

---

[16] It might be pointed out that this book provides a case in point about being skeptical of purported authorities. I am writing from a review and interpretation of the scholarly literature in addition to personal experience as both an instructor and administrator. Thus, the reader is expected to interpret my observations judiciously.

are analogies evidence at all? Well, we often cite examples of something happening as evidence to support a reason. This is on the list of descending quality above formal case studies, lived experiences, and observations from others. All examples have limits related to generating a conclusion from a small sample of observations. Some examples fit the circumstances to support a reason better than others do. Do the examples really apply or are they not applicable? Analogies are like examples of something working in a particular way. One is using the analogy to illustrate a causative process. By avoiding the constraint that one is studying the same phenomenon, one can show how the process may work and thus make a point. Unlike examples, analogies are not suspect due to concerns about generalizing from a small sample. Scientists and critical thinkers of all sorts use analogies on a regular basis. Analogies have powerful explanatory utility. However, one does need to be careful not to overextend, or beg, the analogy. That is, sometimes analogies do not fit the circumstances one is trying to interpret.

The traditional instructor's approach to teaching students about research, and the evidence it produces, is to begin with an explanation of introductory statistics. What is a normal distribution? How does the normal distribution relate to t-tests, analysis of variance, and so on? The traditional assumption is that we are training students to be researchers and we must begin with theory first. The contrarian instructor would disagree. Very few of our undergraduate students will become researchers. All will need to interpret statistics throughout their lives. Students need to develop the tools to interpret the statistics they encounter, only later will a few of them wish to pursue enough statistics to design and execute experiments. The contrarian instructor will concentrate on providing students with the inspiration and tools to develop skill at interpreting the statistics they encounter in critical thinking not in designing the experiments[17].

All of us are inundated with statistical evidence in the media. Usually, someone else has interpreted the statistics for us. The pundits leave out descriptions of the experimental designs, the most significant assumptions in the statistical constructs; as well as the number of subjects or observations, the level of significance, the probability of false positives or false negatives, and on and on. Who paid for the study and why did they spend the money? In

---

[17] The traditional instructor might counter that the people who know how to design experiments are the best at also interpreting the evidence experiments produce. Yes, but it is not practical to expect most people to reach and retain the expertise in designing experiments to allow this approach to work.

media accounts, the interpretations of research findings and statistics are often misleading. It is common for a news reporter to assume that a correlation between two events implies that one caused the other[18]. Some reporter or suave analyst saw a change in the polls happen at the same time as something else and immediately assumed one caused the other. Critical thinking students can develop the tools to assess and challenge such interpretations. All evidence is not created equal and interpreting the evidence is just as important at collecting the evidence. In some cases, it is not practical to know enough to interpret a study described in the media. If one does not know the important factors impacting a research study, one is relying upon the authority of others. The critical thinker will wish to know who the authority is and their skill in interpreting the experimental data.

The much derided concept of intuition is also on the list of viable types of evidence. Under the right circumstances, intuition can be very useful. What if one is forced to make a decision and there is not good evidence of the types higher on the list? The decision is a prediction about something and without specific data for guidance; those with the most experience may be best at making the prediction. Experience counts even if one can't remember having made such a decision before. For example, imagine a physician who has to make a life or death decision. No prior information is available, not even a case study or a testimonial. Yet, if the physician has had experience and practice in a similar environment and knows what is predictable in that environment, and if there was feedback about prior decisions, then that physician is in a much better position to make a guess based on intuition than someone without that background. Kahneman (2011) provides experimental evidence showing that this is clearly the case, and that the success of predictions using intuition is not related to the confidence of the predictors, but only to their experience.

---

[18] There is a logical fallacy in assuming that a correlation between two events implies one caused the other (*cum hoc ergo propter hoc*). One needs a model or theory to imply a causative mechanism from a correlation. For example, one could assert that the population of swashbuckling pirates in the Caribbean Sea has gone down dramatically in the past 300 years. The cost of rum has gone up dramatically during the same time. There would be a high negative correlation. Does that mean that the loss of pirates caused the increase in the price of rum? It is more likely that one could model the pros and cons of running a pirate ship in today's market to explain the decrease in pirates and invoke a separate and unrelated inflationary explanation for the increase in the price of rum.

SIGNIFICANT AMBIGUITY

In many of the physical sciences and in engineering, it is possible to create mathematical models to represent theories and to guide explicit tests of the theories. This is difficult to do in many of the social sciences and just not an option for what is done in the humanities. Verbal expressions are used instead of mathematical models in these fields. It works extremely well. Words are powerful. Yet words have a fundamental ambiguity. Words are slippery things. This ambiguity was recognized by Aristotle as he distinguished between the words and their underlying characteristics. Through the centuries, much scholarship has been directed at semantics, which is the understanding of the use and function of words. Do words come before thoughts or do thoughts create words? In my own discipline, Wendell Johnson did influential work on how the term, stuttering, can influence our reactions to dysfluent speech behaviors. He thought labelling a child as a stutterer caused stuttering[20]. Johnson's studies helped to create the scholarly movement concerned with how differences in words affect our thinking that was termed general semantics (Johnson, 1946). The general semantics movement spread to a large number of universities in the 1950s before being subsumed within linguistics and psychology.

What is the precise meaning of each word and each combination of words we use? In many areas of science, we go to great lengths to get operational definitions explained and controlled explicitly for every variable. Yet, this is not always possible. There is still room for ambiguity and addressing ambiguity is essential as one practices critical thinking. Remember the example given above asserting that it is a fact that "Paris is in France?" That would not be true if the word, Paris, referred to Paris, Arkansas; Paris, Idaho; Paris, Illinois; or Paris, Kentucky. It might, or might not be true, if one were referring to the location of Paris Hilton. In this example, one might consider the ambiguity of "is," "in," and "France." What does it mean to be "in France?" Is France defined by just the land or the space above it too? How much space? Is a satellite orbiting over France in France? If not, then how far below the satellite does something have to be, to be in France? If the buildings, roads, and people that make up Paris are above the surface of the ground, are they in France, or are they above France? For many purposes, legal definitions

---

[20] More recent research has shown that labelling by itself does not cause stuttering, but it is clear that how people talk about disabilities can have powerful influences on behavior.

can help determine things like how far above the land a country extends. In this regard, such explicit definitions are similar to operational definitions used in science.

There is even a great deal of ambiguity in the terminology used in scholarly critical thinking. If there are twelve inches in a foot, is that a fact; or an operational definition? Take the statement: The sun rises every morning. One could assert that the statement is evidence as everyone can witness directly that this happens in their experience, and does so without exception. Yet, not everyone is watching the sunrise every morning. Maybe the statement is more properly considered to be a generalization; that is, a theory. A lot of sunrises have been witnessed and it is reasonable to theorize that the ones that were not observed directly still occurred. Alternatively, maybe the statement about the sun rising is not evidence, but a prediction about the future. Most people would agree that the sun is likely to come up tomorrow and the days beyond. In another example, analogies were listed as a type of evidence in the table above. Yet, one might plausibly assert that analogies are not evidence, they involve theories that one phenomenon has processes parallel to another, yet different, phenomenon.

The point is that all of our critical thinking tools, even the ones that seem the most straightforward; involve some ambiguity. The critical thinker will run into ambiguity in the meaning of words, phrases, sentences, and monologues at every turn; in scholarly arguments as well as the quotidian decisions that direct life directions. One cannot avoid ambiguity. Most of the ambiguity doesn't make a difference. Sometimes though, the slippery meaning of a word or phrase can make a substantial difference in the meaning and subsequent interpretation of an argument. In the jargon used in teaching critical thinking, this is referred to as *significant* ambiguity. I have found that many students have great difficulty recognizing when an ambiguity rises to the level that it is significant in interpreting an argument. Do you agree with the statement that: "Politician X is a great public servant"? Well, it depends on what you mean by "great" and it depends on what you mean by "public servant." In the next chapter we will discuss the concept of confirmation bias and see how ones personal connection to the belief system of the politician will lead to different meanings of these terms[21]. Often, students need reflective practice to pick up

---

[21] Lynne Truss (2006) has written a book on significant ambiguity resulting from poor punctuation, and its title, *Eats, Shoots & Leaves*, comes from the following joke:
"A panda walks into a café. He orders a sandwich, eats it, then draws a gun and proceeds to fire it at the other patrons.

the skill of recognizing significant ambiguity. When the meaning of a word changes in the middle of an argument, it is often referred to as the *equivocation* fallacy.

ASSUMPTIONS

Assumptions are inherent in every action we take and every thought we have throughout our lives. Following up from the ambiguities described above, we make assumptions about the meanings of words and phrases. We also make assumptions that are the initial points of logical departure for every argument. What are the first principles that the author assumes each reader will have in common with them? Often, when examined, many critical thinkers will not agree with an author's assumptions about how the world works or how it should work.

Assumptions are tied to values. Can we assume that others agree with our assessments of what has value, what is important, substantive, or useful? What values do we prefer as a society? Indeed, values are tricky to identify and assess. We could argue about what the common values are for our society, or what they have been in the past, or what they will be in the future. There may not be good answers. Yet, many people writing articles or papers begin their arguments with personal values or world views. Often the value assumptions are opaque with the hubris that others will share them, or if they are hidden, others will just not question them. For example, if a paper is produced by an association with a primary purpose; be it unlimited access to guns, environmental warming, the importance of the coal industry, nuclear disarmament, states' rights, or first-amendment rights; one needs to be vigilant in searching for underlying values assumed by the authors that will color and direct their arguments. Further, many of the arguments we run across are part of conflicts about larger values in our society; e.g., what is the right mix between collective authority and personal freedoms or freedom of the press and national security? The nascent critical thinker will need reflective practice

---

"Why?" asks the confused, surviving waiter amidst the carnage, as the panda makes towards the exit. The panda produces a badly punctuated wildlife manual and tosses it over his shoulder.

"Well, I'm a panda," he says. "Look it up."

The waiter turns to the relevant entry in the manual and, sure enough, finds an explanation. *"Panda. Large black-and-white bear-like mammal, native to China. Eats, shoots and leaves."*

in identifying value preferences and assumptions that are implicit in such arguments.

When I was a university administrator, we developed a program called Critical Thinking about Values. Some people objected to our putting values in such a prominent place in the curriculum. Our response was that university coursework is already full of values (Young, 1997). Think about a biology class. In designing the course, the instructor has most likely assumed that learning about plants and animals is a good thing. It has value. It is also assumed that the material chosen is a fair and appropriate sample of possible material on the topic. The list of assumed values will continue on many levels down to assumptions about each specific assignment, how to spend each class session, or how to deal with problems raised by specific students. My assumption is: The best courses do not advocate for students to change or accept the values inherent in the course, but to develop their critical thinking skills to assess the material and to form value preferences of their own.

LOGICAL FALLACIES

Logical fallacies are another important topic of virtually every course on critical thinking. There are a number of books and treatises devoted to typing and categorizing logical fallacies (Damer, 2005; Gula, 2007). Some of these works are exhaustive with hundreds of different fallacies explained and organized into subgroups. Some of the work is playful and entertaining, such as the many videos on the web by Adam Carolla (2009) lampooning the careless use of the *slippery slope* fallacy. Rather than getting distracted by the richness of this area, I offer my own short table of some of the more common logical fallacies.

Fallacy name	Explanation
Ad hominem	Arguing against the person, not the argument. For example, when a politician labels an opponent with a derisive moniker.
Guilt by association	People I don't like are associated with this idea, so the idea is bad.
Slippery slope	The assumption that making a proposed step will set off an uncontrolled chain reaction when there are many unstated assumptions that may not hold to create such a reaction.
Perfect solution	The assumption that because a solution leaves one part of the problem undone, the solution is not worth doing.

Fallacy name	Explanation
Equivocation or shifting meaning	This is a variation of the concern above for terms that are ambiguous. The ambiguity allows the meaning of a term to change in the middle of the argument.
Ad populum	The assumption that anything preferred by a lot of people is desirable.
Appeal to questionable authority	Assuming that if some person of respect prefers this, then it is worth supporting without reference to their knowledge or reasons. This is also a type of poor evidence.
Appeal to emotion	Using emotionally charged language or threats does not impact the substance of an argument.
Straw person	Taking such an extreme version of the opponent's position that she or he wouldn't support it and then attacking only the extreme elements.
False dilemma, false dichotomy, or either/or	Assuming the answer must be only one of the two alternatives when an additional alternative or a middle ground exists.
Wishful thinking	Assuming that if we wish for something to come true, it will.
Cum hoc, ergo propter hoc	This means: With this, therefore because of this. Yet, when two things happen at the same time it does not mean one caused the other. Correlation does not imply causation.
Post hoc, ergo propter hoc	This means: After this, therefore because of this. Yet, when one thing happens after another thing it does not mean that one causes the other. Correlation does not imply causation.
Glittering generality	Trying to bolster a position by overgeneralization, exaggeration, or hyperbole; and this is more moving when emotionally charged. It just doesn't matter to the substance of the argument.
Red herring	An irrelevant topic or argument is presented as a diversion. This can also be used as a general category containing many more-specific fallacy types.
Tu quoque	This is the hypocrisy fallacy. One tries to dismiss a good argument only because the person advocating it does not follow his or her own advice.
Gambler's fallacy	Losing in the past improves the odds in the future when there is no rationale for expecting this to be the case.
Slammin' or name calling	Attacking an idea by calling it bad words. This is like the ad hominem fallacy, yet one attacks the idea not the person. It is the opposite of the glittering generality fallacy.
Begging the question, tautology	An argument in which the conclusion is assumed in the reasoning. It can also be called circular reasoning. For example, one can give something a name and then argue that it must exist because it has a name.

APPLICATION OF CRITICAL THINKING

The act of critical thinking often takes attention and energy. Sometimes critical thinking is not worth the effort. When one goes to the store to buy a jar of peanut butter, how much critical thinking does one need to employ to choose the best brand? One could make the decision by doing research studies, but that is not practical in most cases. Even reading the labels on the jars and looking up information takes time, attention, and thought. Many of the decisions of our lives are not based on rational calculations. We usually don't want to spend the time and energy on choosing the best peanut butter and even if we did, we are likely to be influenced by social factors more powerful than rational analysis. Clearly, the decisions we make that have the most importance to us should be the ones in which we devote the time and effort for guidance from critical thinking. Each of us may have different values about when that is the case and some people are going to lean toward doing more critical thinking than others. Further, we are often not rational in how and when we use critical thinking and this will be explored in the next chapter.

A related point is that the value of applying critical thinking is not necessarily limited to empirical decisions. John Keats (Scott, 2016) argued that aesthetic decisions still may require what I am calling critical thinking. Beauty is not just in the eye of the beholder--people will often agree on what is beautiful. We can use critical thinking to assess aesthetics, as a judge in an artistic exhibition will attest. The fine and performing arts are clearly established within the realm of scholarship represented in universities. Yet, we don't do well when we try to analyze what makes something beautiful. Typically, we assume that we should spend our efforts with critical thinking when something is important and worth the effort, rather than when it appears research-based or scholarly. This has limits too. When we decide whom to marry, it can be one of the most important decisions of our lives. Does one do a scholarly analysis of the pros and cons of a future spouse, or does one follow ones heart? When should one be rational? Fourteen hundred years ago, St. Benedict implored us to listen with our hearts. He was centuries before much of our scholarship and science, but he had a point[22].

---

[22] A similar point was made by Blaise Pascal: "Le cœur a ses raisons que la raison ne connait point." In English, one translation is: The heart has its reasons; which reason does not know.

Chapter 6

CRITICAL THINKING ABOUT CRITICAL THINKING

In a Harris poll taken in 2013, 42% of 2250 respondents said that they were certain ghosts exist. This is one of many such polls that demonstrate strong belief in the reality of magical or supernatural phenomenon of many sorts. Kida (2006) reviews the prevalence of false beliefs[23]. I have often given a survey of this sort to students in a critical thinking class and the results are similar, if not even higher, for their support of the unbelievable. A lot of time and effort has been devoted to the search for ghosts or other supernatural phenomenon. No substantive evidence has been found. If there were credible evidence, scientists would be on the trail quickly and it would become part of science. Shermer (2011) gives a comprehensive review of circumstances when strange events; e.g., alien abductions, have been reported. Inevitably, these spark a plethora of investigations, but with no findings of anything supernatural. In response to my explaining this in a critical thinking class, the student discussion revolves around how credible the testimonials are of those who have purported to see ghosts and even photograph them. I point out that in the discussion of evidence in the previous chapter, when there is scientific research, it trumps personal testimonials. The students resist. It is a good lesson in the difficulty of learning critical thinking. Perhaps, one of the telling points is that a student once remarked: "It is fun to believe in ghosts. It is fun

---

[23] Kida (2006) makes the case for six basic mistakes we make in our critical thinking: 1) We prefer stories to statistics. 2) We seek to confirm, not to question. 3) We rarely appreciate the role of chance and coincidence in shaping events. 4) We sometimes misperceive the world around us. 5) We tend to oversimplify our thinking. 6) We have faulty memories.

to believe in magic. I love the unicorn who lives under my bed. Don't take that away from me." Yes, magic is awesome. It enriches the esthetic aspects of our lives, keeps dreams alive, and encourages creativity. However, critical thinking can and should be applied to the understanding of magic.

Ricard Dawkins (2011) has written *The Magic of Reality*. It provides direction for how we should go about believing in some things and not others. He explains that magic is one of those slippery, ambiguous words noted in the previous chapter. Magic can mean: 1) supernatural magic, 2) stage magic, and 3) poetic magic.

Supernatural magic is in myths and fairy tales. It is Bilbo Baggins, Harry Potter, and the Wicked Witch of the West. This type of magic is indeed fun to think about. It is a staple of literature, film, and theater. It greatly enriches our lives. But we all know that it is make-believe. It does not really happen.

Stage magic, by contrast, does happen, or at least a magician shows us something that appears to break our understanding of how the natural world is supposed to work. In the case of stage magic, reality appears to be supernatural. The action on stage looks real, or more to the point, it appears to be real given the information the audience has. Most magicians, although they won't tell how their tricks are done, will admit that they are performing tricks. Just like with fairy tales, this type of magic can be fun and entertaining. Unfortunately, there are others who purport to perform magic, like fortune tellers, salespeople peddling magic elixirs, or those who hold séances to communicate with the deceased, who try to trick their victims into believing they really do perform magic. Such charlatans make money through deception. The people who purport to own houses haunted by ghosts and sell you tickets to visit the haunted environs are of this type.

Poetic magic is the magic of reality. There are many wonders in our universe that we can barely begin to understand. The list of wonders that stretch our thinking to the point that it seems both poetic and thrilling is exhaustive: How does the human brain work? How does any brain work? With the theory of evolution, the observations showing that it really does work seem like an absolute wonder even though we have been studying it for 150 years and it is the center of biology[24]. Not only do the numbers of observable stars in the sky seem magical, but the observations from the Hubble telescope have now shown many, many times more stars and galaxies than we ever imagined

---

[24] Interestingly, the Harris poll cited above shows that 42% of the Americans sampled believe in ghosts, also it reports that only 42% of Americans believe in evolution.

before[25]. The poetic magic of our reality is thrilling, as thrilling as any fairy tale or stage magic. But the biggest difference is that supernatural magic and stage magic suspend or defy critical thinking. Poetic magic invites critical thinking and scholarly inquiry to unlock its wonders. Nascent deep learners need to learn to direct their critical thinking skills to unlocking poetic magic and not to be sidetracked by the unexamined claims of other belief systems. Remember the discussion of assumptions and underlying values in the previous chapter? Our tendency to embrace belief systems, especially to fall into the *ad populum* fallacy and take on beliefs of our peers or others who we respect, is one of those hidden values that impact critical thinking. Scholarship is making a considered judgment about who and what to believe.

Why are people so susceptible to accepting false beliefs? Why is it so hard to be rational? Why do we think we are being rational, even when we are not applying critical thinking very assiduously? Why do we need to go to college to hone our critical thinking skills, rather than learning through spontaneous, nonstructured exploration; as when learning to walk and talk? We are humans and our brains operate on principles shaped by millions of years of evolution. We don't operate like robots programmed to be completely rational. As observed by Provine (2012):

> We steer our body through life's straits and shoals, walking, working, talking, speeding up and slowing down, avoiding obstacles. We are the captains of our ship, alert, confident, and rational. That is the illusion. But what if we are deceived by our brain's subtle whispers, its effort, as in dreams, to weave a coherent, sometimes faulty narrative from irrational events? Are we instead unthinking herd animals, driven by subconscious instincts, acting out our species' ancient biological script? (p.12)[26]

What might this ancient script be? Let's back up again to when our primitive ancestors were hunting on the prehistoric savannah. Suddenly there is a rustle in the grass. Is it a saber-tooth cat that would like to eat me? I don't

---

[25] There are purported to be 100 billion galaxies and the galaxies each average around 100 billion stars. The universe is approximately 14 billion years old and Earth didn't exist until about nine billion years ago. These numbers are so extreme that I have a difficult time imagining what they really mean. It is certainly poetic magic.

[26] Perhaps an essential difference between humans and other species was observed my Mark Twain: "Man is the only animal that blushes or needs to." Maybe needing to blush at opportune times, or inopportune times for that matter, is a telling point.

know, but it is better to be safe and run. If I am wrong (a false positive, statisticians would call this a Type I error), the only harm is that I did a little unnecessary running. If I am right, I save my life by running. What if I didn't run? If there were a predatory cat, then I would have made a false-negative mistake (statisticians would call this a Type II error). The cat would eat me. It is naturally much safer to make false positive mistakes. If I am eaten by the cat before I have children, I am out of the hereditary gene pool and future generations will not be like me. These decisions can be characterized in a Pascal square as:

	There is a cat	There is no cat
I run to avoid a cat.	I am right. I save my life and live to benefit the gene pool.	I make a false positive mistake (Type I error). I run, expend energy, and endure a distraction from what I am doing. I benefit the gene pool.
I don't run to avoid a cat.	I make a false negative mistake (Type II error). I am eaten by the cat. I don't procreate so future generations are less likely to think like I do.	I am right. I save a little energy. I benefit the gene pool.

Over the millennia, species have evolved to favor Type I errors. We are leery of cats and snakes in the grass. That was good for survival, but the down side is that if we are biased to imagine what isn't there, we are also prone to believe in ghosts, witches, UFOs, and monsters under the bed[27].

The example of the hunter and the saber-toothed cat came from (Shermer, 2011) who also makes some related points. The propensity to make Type I errors is not just an isolated survival behavior. We are constantly looking for patterns in our world. Our innate thinking tendencies want us to find order and consistency, what Shermer calls *patternicity*. When searching for patterns, and putting a high premium on finding them, we can't help but be on the lookout and make causal inferences when things happen together. This often works, but it also leads to the *cum hoc, ergo propter hoc* (with this then because of this; correlation does not imply causality) logical fallacy.

---

[27] Earlier we discussed some of the different ideas about what really separates humans from other animals. One interesting, if somewhat tongue in cheek, notion is that humans are most different from other animals in their ability and propensity to concoct bizarre belief systems and then to act on the irrational beliefs in rational ways. Do house cats worry about UFOs?

Our bias for identifying patterns and inferring causes, even when they are not there, carries into science. If scientists have a good idea, one that may benefit many people in many ways, they will work hard to demonstrate that the concept is both accurate and predictive. Scientists are prone to want their theories to work, especially if they have invested funding and reputation on the outcome. As a result, scientists are biased to positive outcomes, and thus prone to make Type I errors. The review process in science is geared to accept Type I errors, usually at a P<0.05 level, 5% of the time. Consequently, when a study seems like it should work, scientists continue trying it. One out of 20 times they get a false positive by chance and publish it. The other 19 attempts are not published. Other scientists scan the literature and accumulate large numbers of Type I errors on the topic[28], thus providing a major misunderstanding. As humans, we are prone to accept belief systems.

In addition to patternicity, Shermer explains that we tend to look for *agency*. Agency refers to our tendency to think that things not only happen for a reason, but that somebody else caused them. Was that rustle in the grass caused by something inanimate, like the breeze? Or was there an agent like a fierce cat, a smelly toad, or a ghost? A central theme to much of the fiction we read and many of the movies we watch is that somebody, be it a person or creature, is surreptitiously doing something to somebody. If these agents can do that to others they can do it to us. Agency builds on patternicity, and further primes us to be cautious, circumspect, and suspecting of others; even when the suspects don't exist. We can apply agency to any intriguing sound, vision, or even smell; as somebody or something must be out there. We do this even when we know from critical thinking that giving in to our imagined fears is likely to be a Type I error.

As much as I would love to believe in the ubiquity of critical thinking, true mugwumps are rare. People are just not rational in their thinking or actions much of the time. We evaluate evidence with a bias toward supporting our personal values[29]. There is a substantial body of psychological research showing that this is the case. Three of my favorite summaries of research on biased thinking are Carol Tavris & Elliot Aronson's *Mistakes Were Made (but*

---

[28] This has been termed "p-hacking."

[29] People often follow the *ad populum* fallacy and take on beliefs based on who they are or who they identify with. An acquaintance once remarked: "Our people don't believe that" and what she as commenting upon would be considered self-evident by most people. Denying the veridicality of evidence can also be a way of challenging an authority figure who is associated with the evidence.

not by me): Why We Justify Foolish Beliefs, Bad Decisions, and Hurtful Acts (2007), Keith Stanovich's *What Intelligence Tests Miss: The Psychology of Rational Thought* (2009), and Margaret Heffernan's *Willful Blindness: Why We Ignore the Obvious at Our Peril* (2011).

In Chapter One, I introduced one of the most important principles in this work, the *confirmation bias*. The confirmation bias has been studied extensively for 50 years and shown to be pervasive throughout both scholarly and daily thought and action. Confirmation bias is our propensity to evaluate new evidence to confirm and justify what we already believe or, at least, what is favored by our personal values and identity; and to find reasons to discount what goes against our values. An old aphorism, sometimes referred to as Mile's Law, states: Where you stand on an issue is determined by where you sit (Smith, 2006). What camp are you in already? An expression of confirmation bias is given by the comedian Lenny Bruce as a commentary of the first televised presidential debate. Being more than 50 years old, the politics may seem ancient to some, but perhaps that is good as it removes the example from our own present-day political confirmation biases:

> I would be with a bunch of Kennedy fans watching the debate and their comment would be, "He's really slaughtering Nixon." Then we would all go to another apartment, and the Nixon fans would say, "How do you like the shellacking he gave Kennedy?" And then I realized that each group loved their candidate so that a guy would have to be this blatant—he would have to look into the camera and say: "I am a thief, a crook, do you hear me, I am the worst choice you could ever make for the Presidency!" And even then his following would say, "Now there's an honest man for you. It takes a big guy to admit that. There's the kind of guy we need for President." (From Tavris and Abramson, 2007, p. 18)

As mentioned, the confirmation bias has been studied extensively. It seems to be present everywhere social psychologists look. It is created by our desire to avoid cognitive dissonance. We are uncomfortable with information that challenges a belief, decision, or an aspect of our identity; and we try to minimize the discomfort by challenging and interpreting the evidence to advantage the identify and beliefs in which we have invested. We tend to sharpen and level information as we interpret it. Sharpening means that we emphasize points that fit a bias we have. Leveling minimizes the extraneous information that does not fit our favored points. We all sharpen and level when we report observations or repeat ideas. Sharpening and leveling is uniquitous in the telling and retelling of stories. It is what makes stories more powerful in making the authors' points.

The confirmation bias is amplified by voluntary associations or decisions. If I am walking into a restaurant and I am dismayed to learn that I have to wait a long time for a table, I might like the restaurant less than one with no wait time. If I make a voluntary decision to go to a restaurant and share my expectations of a good experience with others, then when I encounter and endure a long wait, I may be more inclined to appreciate the dining experience more--even if it were identical to the first dinner. We want to justify our actions. If we voluntarily choose to wait, we will be more inclined to like the dinner. We thrive on self-justification and it can easily overcome the logic of critical thinking.

Confirmation bias is also part of our herd mentality. We want to identify with our friends and others who are like us. We take comfort from sharing beliefs with others. We tend to discuss controversial topics with those who agree with us and welcome their expected agreement. Rather than subjecting ideas to critical scrutiny, we tend to embrace the *ad populum* fallacy—this is a popular belief, so it must be true. Cult leaders take advantage of the confirmation bias as well. When people commit to joining a group, they delight in accepting the leader's proclamations; taking them on faith in spite of substantial contradictory evidence (Tavris & Elliott, 2007).

Although social scientists have demonstrated the confirmation bias empirically, there are many observations of its effects through the years prior to its scientific study. There is a traditional facetious axiom: "Never believe in what you can see, if you can believe in what I tell you." In another example, Emily Dickinson wrote the following verse in 1860 (Mackay, 1977, p. 45):

> Faith is a fine invention
> For gentlemen who see;
> But microscopes are prudent
> In an emergency[30].

When one considers it, confirmation bias may not be so destructive. In fact, it has benefits. Take the example of the North American House Hippopotamus. A glossy video on the web exposes a type of secret hippo that is about four inches tall (Concerned Children's Advertisers, 1999). These

---

[30] It was not the practice to use gender neutral language in the 1860s. Also, it should be stressed that Emily Dickinson's use of the term, faith, was in relation to faith in people, not religion.

diminutive hippos interlope in homes across Canada and the Eastern United States by hiding in the depths of littered closets. They build nests of mittens, dryer lint, and bits of string. They sneak out at night to feed on littered chips, raisins, and the crumbs from peanut-butter on toast. These little hippos look like large African hippos, just much smaller and cuter. They are so adorable; you must love them. Do I believe in house hippos immediately? Even the students in my critical thinking classes didn't. The confirmation bias is handy to use to dispel an illogical and fanciful story. The tiny hippos may be cute, but it is not worth the time to take the story seriously. Critical thinking can require a lot of effort and confirmation bias helps protect us from having to use it all of the time.

Further, once we have devoted significant effort to furthering a perspective, value, or world-view; we wish to protect our investment. We will work to distort evidence that challenges beliefs in which we have a stake. Personally, I have invested a lot in the belief that college, research, and scholarship in general, has benefited our world and will continue to do so. If you were to provide evidence to the contrary, explaining that going to college and scholarship were a vacuous squandering of time and resources, my confirmation bias would kick in quickly. Initially I would reject the evidence provided and it would take a lot of substantive information and theoretical prodding before I would be inclined to think objectively about the issue. Perhaps more likely, my confirmation bias would be so strong that challenging evidence would make me dig in my heels rather than softening my position.

My bias about the value of scholarship provides a telling example of how confirmation bias can work on both sides of an argument. Although the value and centrality of scholarship is central to my purposes in fostering liberal education, its value continues to be lost on much of the public and the choices students make. Many people in our society do not turn to scholarship or science, or even critical thinking, when deciding what to believe (Gilovich, 1991; Heffernan, 2011; Shermer, 2011). Forni (2011) makes the point that there is a sense of anti-intellectualism in our society that is uniquely American. He states the "The American ethos may not be easy to define, but one thing it is not is bookish" (p.12). For example, it has been noted that anti-intellectual sentiments play a central role in the debate over global warming (Oreskes & Conway, 2011; Krugman, 2015). Thus, many parents and students may not only fail to appreciate the purpose of critical thinking as embedded in liberal education, but their confirmation bias leads them to oppose it—especially given the high price tag of higher education. Further, many children grow up with the values and beliefs prevalent in their family. Critical thinking is not necessarily a threat to cultural identity, but it can be perceived as such. The confirmation bias can kick in to solidify beliefs to either champion or challenge scholarship—it can work in either direction.

What does an instructor do when dealing with confirmation bias on any topic? The straightforward critical-thinking approach tells us to: Analyze a problem into the issue, reasons, evidence, and so on. Then to recommend a solution and to bolster the solution with even more reasons and evidence. The problem is that the listener may not wish to hear the argument and accept the solutions if it would produce cognitive dissonance. He or she will marshal critical thinking skills to rationalize resistance. Invoking critical thinking to try to overcome a listener's confirmation bias might not be the best approach for two reasons: 1) it doesn't work, and 2) it may even make the listener more resistant. Positive change and learning are thwarted. Stephen Denning (2007) has suggested an alternative approach. To overcome confirmation bias in a group that doesn't agree with you:

- Don't begin with what you think should be done. The confirmation bias will have them resist. Any reasons you give will be rejected.
- Learn about the other group's values, present things in a manner that fits their values.
- Have the other group get to know you and trust you. Have them invest something in believing in you. We value opinions from people we respect.
- Talk about something that needs to be put right. There are problems that need to be solved to make this a better world. These problems are often negative; that is, bad things are happening or going to happen unless action is taken.
- Participate with the other group in developing a vision for a better world leading to a desire for change. This might have been your idea all along, but make them think that they helped develop it. The problems may be presented in the negative, but the anticipated change should promise the positive.
- Only after the positive vision of change is in place do you offer specifics for how to reach the vision. Follow this with reasons why the vision will work.

The approach I am using in writing this book is an example of how to use Denning's advice. I didn't start with asserting that everyone who takes a traditional approach to college instruction is bad and must change. That would have invoked the confirmation bias in many instructors. Instead, I talked about the value of a liberal education and the power of scholarship to make a difference in our world, assuming that many scholarly readers would resonate with such values. The book is purposely personalized and the approach often connects to my own experiences rather than focusing on comprehensively assessing the scholarly literature on what is effective. Instead, I present a problem: Because of the mismatch in purposes between students and instructors, students often put too much effort into pursuing extrinsic goals of education and deep learning suffers. Then there is a vision of a curriculum full of reflective practice that leads to deep learning. Finally, there is discussion of many ways in which readers can use their own talents to foster more deep learning and to get students to become more independent and more mature in their learning. This follows Denning's (2007) advice for how to overcome confirmation bias and get people working together.

We are all familiar with urban legends that never seem to go away. For example: if you leave a lost tooth in a glass of Coke overnight it will dissolve. If you spill Coke on the surface of your car, it will corrode the paint. Indeed, so many urban legends involving Coca Cola exist that the term *cokelore* has been coined. None of the cokelore legends are accurate. Beyond cokelore, our society likes to promote provocative thoughts with little regard to whether the myths are factual or not. I am tired of hearing about the link between vaccines and autism even though the scientific paper associated with that has been found fraudulent and the perpetrator lost his medical license. False stories abound about health care (including nutrition and dieting), child care, politics, celebrity escapades, and most any other topic that comes up. Some of this can be explained in part by confirmation bias, but it seems like the lies often persist in spite of the lack of evidence. As with the discussion of magic and the supernatural, fiction has appeal when parading as something genuine. John Cook & Stephen Lewandowski have studied these lies systematically for years and in 2011 they published a useful guide, *The Debunking Handbook*. It gives a series of steps to combat nettlesome and pernicious myths, that although they are contrarian to the typical scholarly approach of laying out the theory and the evidence, have been shown to be productive:

- Try not to mention the myth, ever. Doing so reinforces its visibility and familiarity. Instead, concentrate on clearly expressing the correct information.
- Keep it simple and concise. A simple myth will persist over a long, comprehensive rebuttal.

- Side-step invoking the confirmation bias. Avoid challenging a world-view or the general values of the persons advocating the myth.
- Fill in the gap. The myth is an explanation, and without it one is left without an answer. It is important to provide a new explanation for what has happened.

There is a lot in common for both the Stephen Denning approach to overcoming confirmation bias and the John Cook and Stephen Lewandowski approach to debunking myths. The point is that as we build and foster critical thinking and scholarship skills in our students, we need to concentrate on leading them to approaches that are effective in promoting scholarly arguments. With all of the hype and marketing in our society, it is easy to be sucked into the herd mentality and not to use critical thinking skills. However, marketing can make a positive difference. When one has substantive points built from sound critical thinking, it is important to market and sell them. Denning (2007) and Cook & Lewandowski (2011) provide us direction for doing so.

Chapter 7

CRITICAL THINKING ABOUT DEEP LEARNING

How does one go about fostering productive deep learning? It turns out that many decades of insightful work done by psychologists have explored exactly that. Good reviews are provided by Brown, Roediger, & McDaniel, 2014; Willingham, 2009; and Carey, 2014. As a contrarian would point out, many aspects of effective learning techniques may be counterintuitive. Because of this, many people don't approach the task of learning in very effective ways. Students need to learn how to learn more effectively in school. Many instructors take a scholarly approach to the content of their courses, but remain unaware of the substantial scholarly evidence about what makes a learning experience most effective. Just like with the rumors, legends, and belief systems discussed in the previous chapter, misconceptions about learning need to be debunked.

Sometimes even when students are out of school they do use effective deep learning strategies to pursue their interests. Teenagers can often be curious. Many teenagers thrive on being skeptical. They ask and answer their own questions as a deep learner. But then when these same individuals get into a school-like environment, they are experienced at becoming passive and subservient to the instructor. A distinguished guest at my university once gave a presentation on music education. He made the point that kids in kindergarten are often active, outgoing, and anxious to participate in any learning activity. In music class they want to bang on every drum, toot on every horn, and just try every instrument. Through the years, the kids learn discipline and restraint, but it comes with a price. The price is that they do not expect that their own curiosity belongs in the classroom. The kids learn to sit quietly, do what they are told to do, and finish any thinking task by confirming what they are told to conclude. One might conjecture that years of formal schooling would increase curiosity and the quest for understanding and inspiration. Instead, the system rewards students for thinking what they are told to think and doing what they are told to do. Instructors tell students how science works, how the world works. Students, as surface or strategic learners, think they are to reiterate the instructors' assertions back on tests. Instructors are authorities on the content and they have authority related to classroom behavior--so students assume they should accept what instructors say and not challenge it. As educators, it is easy to forget that our primary goal should be getting students to be asking their own questions and to work hard to answer them. Students are poor judges of what they are learning, and it is easy for them to slide into surface and strategic learning that relies on instructors judging them. Students do not realize, or they forget, that this is their opportunity to sharpen their learning skills. The bottom line is that learning in pursuit of ones own interests, because one has curiosity leading to compelling questions, is central to deep learning. It should be the primary goal for instructors leading students or anyone else[31].

Thinking is hard work. It takes effort. As I am writing this book, I am constantly coming up with reasons to do something else. I procrastinate. Why? Although thinking can be exhilarating and rewarding, it is also challenging. We like to do what we are doing most of the time--and that is not thinking too much. Remember the example of not wanting to exert the effort of critical thinking for choosing a brand of peanut butter at the store? One could get lost in web-searches of the various ingredients, their nutritional value, and long diatribes about health risks; which may or may not be fallacious or at least slanted by confirmation bias. How do we assess value of one peanut butter brand over another? It is easiest to pick a favorite or familiar brand off of the shelf and trust that the taste and quality will be acceptable. The important thing to remember about learning is that it is integrally tied to cognitive effort. The amount we learn depends on how hard, and how creatively, we are thinking about the material. How good are the questions we are asking? Any of us could learn a great deal about peanut butter if that were desired. Peanut butter evaluation could be an area of scholarly interest. But it takes mental effort and the time, ability, and resources to collect information. Is peanut butter worth

---

[31] I think this relates to an earlier issue, what makes humans different from other animals and why are humans here on Earth? What is our destiny? If our most human characteristic is the ability to dream of a better world, then it may be no surprise that having our own questions is a powerful motivator in driving deep learning.

that? There are no shortcuts to critical thinking. It takes time. It takes attention. It takes energy. Time, attention, and energy are valuable resources. There are times when peanut butter evaluation might be worth the price, but for most of us it isn't.

Unfortunately, students have many misconceptions about learning (Chew, 2014). We have already dealt with some of them; for example, students confuse deep learning and strategic learning. Students often do not distinguish between intrinsic and extrinsic rewards in relation to learning. As a consequence, students have a misconception that getting the answers right on the test or getting a good grade should be their goal for a course. Students also tend to think that the process of learning is to file away isolated facts for future retrieval from the mental filing cabinet. Although one has to remember some material to direct reflection and performance, the heart of knowledge is knowing how to use the information one has and to get the information one doesn't. Students don't understand that the goal is developing the facility to be able to learn to do new things more effectively. Further, learning is exercising far transfer of skills developed in class to thinking and acting outside the course. Yet, students often spend far too little time and effort trying to use skills they have learned in their classes outside of class. For example, students often learn to do projects in a physics or mechanics class that apply Newton's Laws of Motion. Unfortunately, when queried outside of class they don't realize they could use these laws to solve problems somewhat different from those encountered in class.

The paragraph above talked about how learning is related to thinking. One has to think to learn and the more effort put into thinking, the more understanding one gets. A common student misconception is that they underestimate how much time and energy critical thinking, and learning in general, consumes. Students seldom allow themselves enough time for deep learning. In this regard, another misconception is that students believe they are good at critical thinking, yet it is clear that they need to learn and refine their skills at critical thinking. Willingham (2009) has reviewed the evidence that shows people are poor judges of what they know and understand.

Another misconception about learning is that students often feel it is easier to learn in content areas that fit their personal interests. A great deal of psychological research shows that learning is most facilitated by the intrinsic rewards of problem-solving (Willingham, 2009). Problem-solving is asking questions and answering them. It is what makes things interesting. Content can be interesting initially, but it gets stale without new challenges. Consider crossword puzzles or jigsaw puzzles. People are drawn to work on them.

Puzzlers spend hours thinking about the words or the pieces of the picture. Yet, there is very little content in these puzzles. The words don't mean much in a crossword puzzle. The picture in a jigsaw puzzle may be nice to look at when done, but hardly so much so that one would toil away for hours in figuring out how the pieces fit together just to look at the finished picture. The intrinsic reward of reaching the challenge of completing a jigsaw puzzle is much more influential.

The crux of this discussion is that students can learn to become interested in any material, if it is introduced in the right way, with the right sequence of challenging puzzles for the reflective practitioner to solve. Here is an example: In a documentary I saw on the medieval Vikings, there was an interview with an anthropology professor who loved human feces. He giggled with delight over a fossilized turd, termed a coprolite, from the Vikings. The professor was enamored by the way one could induce the Vikings' hunting, diet, and cooking habits from this coprolite. Was this individual initially a scatologist prior to becoming an anthropologist? I doubt it. He learned his fascination with feces from a significant amount of puzzle solving in the context of reflective practice. The point is that one can even learn to love shit.

What is meant when one says that an instructor is an interesting lecturer? One interpretation is that this instructor is entertaining. Such lectures are filled with jokes, surprises, and maybe even some intriguing tricks. Or lectures can project a pleasant, often revered, presentation style that makes the listeners comfortable and reassured. Unfortunately, such lectures do not necessarily lead to more deep learning. In fact, when queried later the students often remember the jokes and fun moments of the class or admiration for the instructor, not the point of the lectures. In my first college biology course, the instructor often surprised us by pulling lab mice, lizards, and other small animals out of his coat pocket. That is what I remember about the class. It was fun and reassuring, but it did not necessarily inspire me to ask my own questions[32].

Another way in which we talk about a class being interesting is that it connects with what a student already cares about. This can be useful if a student is attracted by the topic in a way that creates a deep learning mode right away. However, prior interest is not necessary. The anthropologist mentioned above had learned to love shit. Courses can become attractive to

---

[32] An unexpected twist can make an impression that will enhance the likelihood it will be remembered. But the instructor should ensure that the point to remember is connected to the larger issues and worth remembering.

students even without antecedent attraction to an area. This is done by filling the course with activities in which problems are challenging to the students. Just like with puzzles and games, especially as discussed in the next chapter on video games, the challenges have to fit the capacities of the learner. If problems are too hard, students get frustrated. If problems are too easy, students get bored. This relates to a traditional psychological concept called Vygotsky's (1978) *zone of proximal development*—one develops by meeting challenges designed at the right level. The challenges are not too hard. The challenges are not too easy. Goldilocks might note the challenges are at the level to provide the expectation that the effort necessary for critical thinking will be worth it. The larger point is if one can design learning experiences with the right amount of challenge for problem solving, students can enjoy learning even without any prior expectation that they would find the material interesting[33]. In contrast, what isn't much fun is to sit in a class and passively write down notes during a lecture. If one wants to be passive, today's media options offer much more in terms of one-directional, noninteractive entertainment.

All learning requires prior knowledge, so instructors should think about what students already know and connect to it when designing classes and learning experiences. The specifics of the content presented are not as important as what the content will mean to the students when they begin to build on it from their prior knowledge. One can't just fill students' heads with the content. Students need to interpret material for themselves and decide what it means to them. How does an instructor direct students to search for personal meaning and to have that search direct the extraction and interpretation of key ideas? Scholarly content is an important foundation for each class, but the instructor needs to think much less about presenting new facts and new perspectives, and to think much more about how any new material will be the stimulus to help students build a foundation from what they already know or believe. This is more challenging for an instructor than one might assume. Through the years I have asked many instructors to describe the material they cover in a class. They do so with enthusiasm. When queried about what it will mean to the students, they defer to the goal that the students will understand their points and remember them. Instructors have difficulty grappling with the idea that the material is there not so much for the students to understand, but

---

[33] There is a message here for designing lectures. It is more important to be clear and appropriately challenging than it is to be entertaining. In fact, entertainment can interfere with deep learning.

primarily to stimulate the students to ask and seek their own questions. When I ask: What questions does this material lead your students to develop? Too many instructors stare at me blankly, or more typically, they just tell me more about the content they cover. I am reminded of teaching a dog to whistle.

Students are also under the mistaken notion that mass practice works. It doesn't. Rereading something or going over and over it to memorize material for an examination is not very effective. It lacks the interest of being invested in one's own questions and the challenge of problem solving. Mass practice may lead to some near transfer, but little far transfer. Even active practice, not just reading or listing but doing something with the information over and over such as retrieval with flash cards, doesn't help much. Spaced practice is more efficient than massed practice. Spaced practice forces one to recall and refresh skills, so the processes that make spaced practice work also make it more effective than mass practice for long-term learning. The point is that mixing up mass practice in time and application helps, but not enough. Although the term practice is used, reflective practice is distinctly different from mass, spaced, or even active practice. In reflective practice the emphasis is having the practitioner analyze what is being done, ask his or her own questions, and answer them. Reflective practice does have a lot of repetition, but the idea is to reflect and think critically on what is being done over and over in slightly new circumstances.

Further Willingham (2009) explains that mass practice is terrible for motivation. If you want to learn to hate something, be forced to do it over and over without variation. What helps most for both motivation and for far transfer is caring about making it work in all sorts of new situations. That comes with caring about ones own questions and the intrinsic rewards of solving puzzles. Think again of the example of the apprentice learning a trade by honing skills through reflective practice over a long period of time—the process mixes up the learning. One is constantly asking questions, reflecting, critical thinking, and problem solving.

Some people prefer visual instruction, others want it verbally. Yet, a significant amount of research shows that it is not necessarily better to use a preferred modality to learn something. More often it is better to use many modalities. A related misunderstanding is that students and many instructors think that long, detailed instructions will facilitate learning and problem solving. In many situations learning is facilitated by minimizing instruction and allowing students to discover and figure things out on their own. Asking and answering one's own questions about how to do a task is better than working on someone else's questions. This will be discussed in more depth in the next chapter on video games.

Students and instructors also commonly have misunderstandings about testing. The role of testing as a learning tool will be explored further in Chapter Nine. Testing can mislead students if they think it is primarily summative; that its purpose is to grade their accomplishments in comparison to meeting minimum standards or to compare them to other students. This reinforces surface or strategic learning behaviors. The larger point here is that students in surface and strategic learning mode do not realize that testing is primarily a learning experience. Testing can be formative. Testing is the students' opportunity to practice solving puzzles under pressure and to get feedback on how well they are learning. Students can compare how effective different efforts on their part are in enhancing their learning skills. Often students don't realize testing doesn't need to be formal. Any time one is practicing a skill, one can examine how well he or she is doing.

Strategic learners never want to get a test item wrong. Yet, mistakes, errors, and wrong answers on tests are useful. Testing can be good as a form of, not just calibration, but of feedback. When we make a mistake, we can analyze. We can try again. We can make adjustments until we figure out what works. Mistakes are good in that they are part of problem solving; that is, asking and attempting to answer questions. There is a, probably apocryphal, story about Thomas Edison. He was criticized for trying and failing in 100 different experiments to find an element that would allow a light bulb to shine. His response was that the 100 wrong guesses were not errors, but a learning process that eventually led him to effective solutions. The contrarian would point out that if one misses a number of questions on a test, but responds by learning from the wrong answers, then it was better than getting all the answers correct initially. Getting all of the answers right is not a learning activity from a formative standpoint. Deep learners might realize getting all the answers correct is a waste of time. Of course, the strategic learners love it.

I have already talked a good deal about student's attitudes and conceptions about learning. The work of developmental psychologist Carol Dweck and her colleagues provides yet one more important misunderstanding that can be related to student attitudes—*fixed-entity* learning versus *incremental-entity* learning. It is easy for students to think they are just naturally good at some learning tasks and more challenged in others. Their notion is that learning is a relatively stable skill, a fixed entity. An individual is either good at playing chess or not, depending on ones natural ability (Waitzkin, 2007). In contrast, other students might take an incremental learning approach. They understand that learning follows a long course of development and if they work diligently enough at something, like playing chess or critical thinking, even the most difficult skills can be learned incrementally.

Dweck and colleagues (Ellliott & Dweck, 1988; Mangels et al., 2006) have shown that students who think learning is a fixed entity will tend to become frustrated. The students think they are either talented or not and so there is little they can do about it. If they are not talented they perform poorly. If they are talented, they become overconfident and less talented students who work hard catch up with them. How frustrating. Waitzkin (2007) refers to this as a learned helplessness. Unfortunately, our society often accepts a fixed entity approach. For example, I have heard people announce to others in social gatherings: "I don't do math." They say this in a way that implies they were just not born with math ability. They feel no need to apologize for not putting in the effort to learn to do math[34]. In contrast, other people understand the incremental nature of learning. They seek out mastery of new skills and work hard. They are the ones prone to deep learning. It is the responsibility of instructors not to let students get caught up in the frustration of the fixed-entity approach. However, remember the discussion of debunking myths and overcoming confirmation bias in the previous chapters? It is difficult to free students from the defeatism promulgated by the fixed-entity myth about learning, although Dweck and colleagues have shown that it can be done through procedures similar to what is referred to here as reflective practice. Perhaps following the ideas of Denning (2007) and Cook & Lewandowsky (2011), discussed above in Chapter Six, will help as well.

A final student misconception discussed by Chew (2014) is that students often believe they are good at multitasking[35]; that is, doing many activities at once like studying and listening to music. But remember, learning takes thinking. Thinking takes attention and any other task will take our attention

---

[34] A great many people live with learning disabilities that can impact math skills that need to be understood and dealt with professionally. However, it is my assertion that the number of people who are math adverse, and yet don't seem to understand that it is their own shortcoming, is greater than the number of us who have learning disabilities and who have worked diligently to overcome their challenges, some being more successful than others. On a related note, our society is much less accepting of persons with a fixed entity approach to reading. There is a stigma with reading disabilities. One is not likely to hear a person announce to a group: "I don't read." Yet, math and literacy are similar in the regard that many individuals do have to overcome significant learning disabilities, but we all can learn from repeated and meaningful instruction and effort.

[35] Of course, they could take either a fixed-entity or incremental-entity approach to mastering multitasking. Were they just born good at it or have they honed the skill?

away from the learning. It has been shown that people can only attend to one thing at a time (Kahneman, 2011). What is referred to as multitasking is really switching attention rapidly among competing tasks. A number of studies demonstrate that attempting to multitask impacts ones performance in learning (Sanbonmatsu, Strayer, Medeiros-Ward, & Watson, 2013). The only times when multitasking does not decrease learning is when the secondary tasks can be done so automatically that they do not require much attention[36]. Students may think they are multitasking when listening to music while studying. If the background music is not impacting attention, it may as well not be there. Other tasks can become so automatic that people can do them without much competition for their attention. For example, we can walk and talk at the same time. Both skills take a great amount of neural processing and skill development. However, they are so highly practiced that we can easily switch attention between them when necessary. Interestingly, when one learns to drive a car most of the tasks are new. It takes full attention to drive when one is initially learning. When one becomes a skilled driver, it can take much less attention and one can easily switch among three tasks: driving, listening to the radio, and singing along at the same time[37]. The point is that learning anything takes direct attention. The more clearly one can focus attention, and put in the mental effort to think, the more one can set the stage for learning.

What can we do about these student misconceptions? As mentioned above, some of them are related to persistent myths or they invoke confirmation biases about a student's self-concept. Whatever, the case, we need to use the approaches explained by Denning (2007) and Cook & Lewandowsky (2011) in Chapter Six to combat them. If instructors care about deep student learning, then it is their obligation to organize opportunities to allow students to work through them. Are these biases typically considered when we design learning experiences? Do we ignore them? Do we mention them in class in a way that invokes resistance from confirmation bias, or in a way that offers a positive new vision and solutions? Do we get students to ask and test their own questions about them? Asking such questions might not just lead to more deep learning, the deep learning might have intrinsic rewards that would reinforce even more improvement in learning skills.

---

[36] Kahneman (2011) develops the distinction between fast, automatic thinking that he calls system I, and slow, deliberate thinking, referred to as system II. Clearly learning is system II thinking and involves full attention.

[37] But don't text and drive, that takes too much attention-sharing to be safe.

Chapter 8

USING VIDEO GAMES AS A GUIDE
TO INSPIRE DEEP LEARNING

What would most students rather do: 1) go to a lecture, 2) do their homework, 3) watch or participate in an athletic event, or 4) play any other type of game? Perhaps, you weighed the merits of choices three or four and quickly dismissed the first two options. Few of us think that students want to go to class or study assignments rather than participate in what they see as more fun and attractive, items three and four, sports and games. Lectures and homework are seen as work. Games are seen as fun. Why is that? One idea is that sports and games are based on fundamental human attributes; such as finding the right mix of challenge, curiosity, competition, and cooperation; and that they have been developed and refined over thousands of years (Koster, 2005; McGonigal, 2011). As explained in Chapter Seven we like the rewards of solving crossword and jigsaw puzzles. Many other games, like chess, bridge, and tennis have shown a lasting attraction. The games that have the right mix of attributes persist. Refinements that make them more attractive are often adopted (Manrique, 2013) so over the years the games get better. Games tap into a part of human nature that is fundamental, like relationships or the desire to win, even if the victory is only symbolic as it is with many games and sports. We have a desire to make a difference with our lives and the victories inherent in games symbolize meaningful accomplishments, even when there is no prize money or other tangible outcome[38]. Good games are challenging and

---

[38] The idea that we are driven to make a lasting difference with our lives might also be thought of as one of the things that distinguishes humans from other animals. As with other animals we

rewarding. As with Vygotsky's zone of proximal development, the successful games are not too hard and they are not too easy. They have the right level of challenge so we are motivated to work for success.

When the deep learner approaches a topic, it is a lot like a game. Can she or he reach insights and then apply those insights for the success of solving a puzzle? Why isn't this a universally recognized part of education? Why don't we all love to come to class to enter into the game of learning? A pundit enamored with active learning might say that the problem is that classes are just lectures. Lectures are one-directional and as the students take notes and try to remember the professors' insights, they are not playing a game. Remember the parable about the prehistoric hunter-gatherer societies and reflective practice? During the day, a young child is learning to hunt with a parent. The child practices tracking, stalking, and spear throwing as a good reflective practitioner would do. Yet, when the child comes home at night and the clan sits around the campfire, the elders tell stories of great hunts and the clever ways they were successful. In a way, these stories reflect the victories of successful problem solving. Reflective practice can be followed up by storytelling. Interestingly, storytelling is at the heart of many games, especially video games. As with the campfire stories, the video games connect the story to the actions of the participant. Storytelling is also at the heart of giving a good lecture. However, too many lectures do not connect to the reflective practice of the student. The great lecturers of today, the ones that stimulate the deep thinkers to ask their own questions, are the ones that build on an ancient tradition of storytelling, but do so to complement the problem-solving of the

---

want to improve the world by bringing up well-reared offspring, and we hope and expect our children will do more to improve the world than we do. Yet, humans are unique in their desire to contribute to science and the understanding of our world, literature and the arts in general. What other animals want to contribute to esthetic insights, as well as to make societal contributions that will advance and protect society as well as the condition of our Earth in general? Here is a quote from Albert Einstein (1954) that makes me think along these lines:

> Only the individual can think, and thereby create new values for society, nay, even set up new moral standards to which the life of the community conforms. Without creative personalities able to think and judge independently, the upward development of society is as unthinkable as the development of the community. ... there is such a thing as a spirit of the times, an attitude of mind characteristic of a particular generation, which is passed on from individual to individual and gives its distinctive mark to a society. Each of us has to do his little bit toward transforming this spirit of the times. ... Let every man judge by himself, by what he has himself read, not by what others tell him.

reflective practitioner. In video games as well as in hunting and college learning, practice comes first, stories direct and build on what has been practiced, and explanations about theory come only when needed to solve a puzzle.

One could point to the appeal and popularity of many different types of games and sports. Many of us are captivated by games and they form important influences in society. But some games, like video games, are often criticized as a waste of time or even worse, attracting children with violent or adult content. Yet video games have been extremely popular. Even though the impact of computer technology has been difficult to predict over the past few decades, it is clear that video games have exceeded expectations. In 2012, the video game industry grossed over $20 billion (Entertainment Software Association, 2014). Video games are played around the world for more than three billion hours a week (Knewton Inc., 2014). The average player will devote around eight hours a week and many players put in much more time than that (Entertainment Software Association, 2014)[39]. Players are motivated to work hard and to concentrate for sustained periods of time. They are motivated to learn many detailed facts, insights, and tricks for playing any game. Players can have difficulty putting a game down, even when mentally fatigued (Beck & Wade, 2004). Can the same thing be said for how students approach their educational experiences? For the deep learner, yes. But video games reach many individuals who do not take a deep learning approach to much of their education. How can we design our educational experiences to incorporate these fundamental aspects of human nature, to create interest in searching for more insight, and to compel students to commit themselves to deep learning? We know that just putting more background information, theory, or even jokes into a lecture won't do it. We can include the charm of storytelling in our lectures, but more than that, how can we build the attraction of game playing into students' educational experiences? First we need to identify what encourages and fosters deep learning in games, and then we can consider how to get students to use them when addressing scholarly content.

Over the past few years, there has been a move to take game design principles and apply them to nongame situations, which is called gamification.

---

[39] Interestingly, video games have an appeal that is wider than some might think. For example, Shapiro (2015) notes "While 60% of American adults believe that 'most people who play games are men,' gender actually has little to do with whether or not you game: A nearly identical share of men and women report ever playing video games (50% of men and 48% of women)."

Knapp (2012) explains that gamification is "using gamed-based mechanics, aesthetics, and game thinking to engage people, motivate action, promote learning, and solve problems" (p. 10). Knapp (2012) reviewed the interest in applying gamification to business and industry with examples from marketing, training, employee satisfaction, employee health, and social change. Much of the interest in gamification has been devoted to improving education (Schaffer et al, 2005); for example, Gee (2007) has developed 36 different principles inherent in video games that he has applied to ideas for improving student learning in school. Aldrich (2009) has emphasized that the aspects of gamification that have been successful in education are those which involve procedural learning. That is, students learn facts only in the context of figuring out how to analyze and act in a situation. They are learning how to perform as a skilled participant or professional, just as Schön (1983) would propose for the reflective practitioner.

In general, the successful design principles of video games incorporate the motivational principles found in many traditional games (Chatfield, 2010, Knapp, 2012; McGonigal, 2011). However, there are a number of different ideas about what makes a video game successful, and there are many varying lists of effective principles (Lecky-Thompson, 2007; Rogers, 2010; Schell, 2008). Further, different games may incorporate different principles to a different extent. Although a broad pool of game design principles could be explored for their impact on student learning (Gee, 2007), in this chapter I will review six examples: 1) the essential-experience principle, 2) the discovery principle, 3) the risk-taking principle, 4) the generalization principle, 5) the reward-system principle, and 6) the identity principle. I am choosing these principles primarily because I am most familiar with them as they formed the basis of a paper on video games and therapy design in speech-language pathology by Folkins, Brackenbury, Krause, & Haviland (2016)[40]. It should be emphasized that these six principles are exemplars of gaming in general. They are not an exhaustive list of the principles of video games that motivate deep learning; but they do center on fundamental aspects of the educational process such as challenging the student, far transfer of insights, fostering creativity, providing feedback, and balancing intrinsic and extrinsic reward systems.

---

[40] The paper by Folkins et al. (2016) might be of interest to many of the readers of this book, even those not interested in, or familiar with, speech-language pathology, as it includes more explanation of the video design principles discussed along with more specific documentation of sources.

THE ESSENTIAL-EXPERIENCE PRINCIPLE

There is a difference between the mechanics of playing a video game and the overall experience of playing it. The mechanics include the characters, storyline, visual design, and manipulation of the hardware. The overall experience, referred to by Schell (2008) as the essential experience, includes all of the mechanics as well as all of the thoughts and emotions a player has while engaged in the game; that is, how they are perceiving and interpreting the overall impressions of their experience. Gee (2007) refers to this same principle as a game's systems thinking and Squire (2011) discusses it as the ideological world of the game. Different video games may have entirely different essential experiences for the player. For example, one video game might emphasize the thrill of hunting or being hunted, another game might focus on the delight of developing and implementing complex strategies for creating an empire. In well-constructed video games, the different design elements of the game help to support the essential experience. A good designer might identify an essential experience first and then build the game around support for that experience; however, the essential experience might not always be the initial part of creating the game, it might emerge from a thoughtfully integrated combination of experiences.

Minecraft (Mojang, 2011) is an example of a video game in which the essential experience is to explore in tactful and creative ways. No central goals are given initially and players manipulate the game's vast landscape to see what might happen as they explore a mine. They manipulate raw materials into tools to create structures. Players can share and build in the worlds of other players. Motivation is inherent in this creative problem solving. The essential experience of Minecraft builds on exactly what motivates the deep learner[41].

When we design a college class, how often do we think about the essential experience for the students? Too often the instructor thinks first about what material will be covered and how deeply or comprehensively to deal with it within the confines of one course. It is easy for a traditional instructor to assume that the student will connect to the material with respect and appreciation for it in the way that the instructor already does. However, too often that is not the essential experience for the student. On a lecture by lecture

---

[41] An example of a video game is given for the essential experience principle. Examples have not been included for the other five principles reviewed below, but the interested reader can find example games explained in Folkins, Brackenbury, Krause, & Haviland (2016).

basis, does the student leave class with the stimulation of the deep learner, who is excited and motivated to explore more about the day's topics? Or was the student's experience one of watching the clock for the hour to be over and he or she could quit taking notes? When playing video games, players are not typically watching the clock and looking forward to when they can quit.

Instructors can and should consider the students' experience not just in the lecture, but in the class as a whole. When students reflect on the lectures, plus the readings, homework assignments, special projects, and all of the rest; what happens? Do the students just reflect on the content or do they realize that the content was embedded in the larger goals of the course or the curriculum? Maybe the students do not need to recognize this, but as instructors, we should to be cognizant of the larger goals. What are the essential experiences for the students and how can we align them with the essential experiences that make up a liberal education? Can we design classes that build passion to learn more about a content area? Can we design classes with an essential experience that reinforces the joy of scholarship? Can we design classes that build critical thinking skills and reinforce the desire to use them? Can we design classes that encourage deep learning? Can we design classes that stimulate the desire to be creative and make a difference in the world?

Through the years, I have witnessed students gaining different essential experiences. Many students have the strategic learner experience. They take pride in their accomplishments on tests and assignments, as well as their grades. In their eyes, they are playing the education game and winning. They are winning, but they have the essential experience wrong. Unfortunately, these students outnumber the students who are the deep learners; that is, the students who are excited and motivated not just to learn more on their own, but to go out and make a difference in the world with their new-found insights.

THE DISCOVERY PRINCIPLE

When someone tells us something, it is easy to forget it. When we have our own questions and need to seek out the answers, we tend to remember those answers (Alfieri, Brooks, & Aldrich, 2011). The discovery principle is the idea that we should promote learning through asking our own questions and discovering the answers. We can begin with an example. Imagine that you go online and purchase a high-tech, multiphase, revolving widget. This widget is supposed to do many fantastic things. The box arrives and you open it. The widget is covered with a host of controls: buttons, dials, switches, and levers;

perhaps today though the widget would have no controls, just a way to enter commands. How does one use it? The traditional approach would be to go to the manual and read it thoroughly before even touching the widget. Then slowly follow the step-by-step instructions for startup. What a chore. It is especially frustrating when the steps do not work quite right or there is ambiguity in what to do when. It is much more fun, and productive, to start pressing buttons and turning dials. The traditionalist might voice an alert that the widget could be damaged. Yes, but that is usually not a concern. The larger point is that when we are exploring the widget for ourselves, we are solving a puzzle. There is a challenge that is manageable and we feel good meeting it. There is an intrinsic reward in seeing the widget perform its useful functions. This is the discovery principle and it relates directly to Schön's reflective practice.

Following the discovery principle, video games don't include instruction manuals. The manuals are as boring as a college lecture. It is not only difficult to find a video game with any instructions, this is the case also for computers, tablets, and smart phones. The instructions are not desired or expected by most users of electronic devices. One can find answers online to any question when one needs the answer. It is not desirable to wade through a recondite manual first. Just open the game or other application and start exploring. Games are designed for the players to enjoy discovering how to use them.

The discovery principle can be seen, not just for the new player seeking initial instruction, but throughout the decisions made in playing many video games. In addition to directing players to discover how to succeed in the game, video games provide a rich environment that immerses players in complex situations containing clues and suggestions about where to look for the answers. The early video games had yet to incorporate fully the discovery principle, they often gave explicit instructions during play and there tended to be only a few circumscribed routes to win the game. As explained by Rogers (2010), instead of providing only limited options and abilities throughout, now video games are designed so that as the play progresses the players solve puzzles that reward correct responses with new skills. Players use critical thinking skills to not only figure out how to play, but to learn from previous experiences, and progressively build the skills and abilities to become successful (Shaffer et al., 2005). Games are built on the intrinsic motivation derived from discovering solutions. The more contemporary video games minimize instruction and provide many routes to discovery, thus stimulating creativity. It is fun to be creative.

This is the opposite of the approach many traditional instructors take to designing their classes. Typically, the traditional instructor lays out the theory first. That is, traditional instructors begin with explanation of the reasons for how things work as they do. Then they give examples. The students take notes passively. Students are listening and writing, but they are not discovering. Then the traditional instructor may provide activities for students to apply the theory to solving prescribed problems with set answers. Creativity and discovery is often not as important in such exercises as following directions, calculating correctly, and giving ample attention to detail. Too often the traditional problem solving exercises are on the level of the early video games. Yet, few things embody deep learning as much as the thrill and intrinsic rewards of discovery.

THE REWARD-SYSTEM PRINCIPLE

Many video games provide excellent examples of how extrinsic reward systems should work. They have built-in rewards that are specific to the level and accomplishments of the player. The games give frequent feedback. They are explicit in signaling ongoing achievement. In video games, the extrinsic reward systems are often referred to as pointification. They include not only points, but praise, badges, new resources, accumulated powers, and advancement to the next level (Schell, 2008). The extrinsic rewards can also be negative, such as punishments, loss of points, loss of lives or powers, or additional challenges that need to be met. Yet, video games use the extrinsic reward systems to promote desired behaviors that lead to intrinsic rewards, such as gaining better mastery of the game mechanics, spending more time concentrating on and progressing with the game, enjoying oneself, and even recommending the game to others. The fundamental issue is how to organize the game so that the extrinsic rewards directly lead to the intrinsic rewards, and that the players recognize that the intrinsic rewards are the most meaningful as they directly contribute to the essential experience of the game. In the end, the points and badges don't mean as much as the personal rewards the players get from their participation. If this were not the case, people would not bother to play the game for the meaningless extrinsic rewards.

The reward system relates directly to the discussion about strategic and deep learning. In many class experiences, the strategic learners are fixated on the extrinsic rewards of test scores, grades, and advancement to the next level. They do not connect these extrinsic rewards to the reasons why they are in school. They are doing what is assigned rather than learning to take responsibility for what they are learning. As pointed out previously, in many cases there is concern that the obsession with the extrinsic rewards of our educational systems can hide and suppress the intrinsic rewards of becoming a mature and powerful learner. In contrast, many video games are designed so that one needs to develop an appreciation, perhaps not necessarily consciously, for the intrinsic rewards of playing. In traditional classes, there can be too much emphasis on accumulation of information and responding in ways that the students expect the instructor wishes. How can we ensure that our extrinsic reward systems are built to create more recognition and intrinsic rewards for refining and polishing critical thinking skills, driving ones curiosity, or creating new insights?

THE RISK-TAKING PRINCIPLE

Sometimes we like to take risks; for example, people often like to gamble. Other times we try to avoid exposure to risks; for example, strategic learners want to meet every requirement and do not wish to risk even a small chance of failure. It is easy to feel tense and uncomfortable in risk-adverse situations. In contrast, people are often comfortable in, and attracted to, climates in which the rewards are recognizable, not necessarily large or tangible, but explicit and understood; and losses are manageable. It is fun to play games of chance of many sorts. Video game designers understand that achievements and other rewards discussed above in the reward system principle should not be too predictable, because the element of chance adds to the thrill of winning and the hope of winning can be a powerful motivator. Winning when there is risk is very related to the act of searching for, and finding, rewards in the discovery principle. Thus video games are designed to offer a variety of challenges providing a balance between recognized rewards and manageable risks. Just as with Vygotsky's (1978) zone of proximal development, the risks embedded in video games must be formulated to be challenging enough to be solvable but not too easy. As explained in the reward system principle, some of the rewards earned in video games are extrinsic. They are points, badges, and stars. Designers of more contemporary video games have recognized that they can build useful extrinsic rewards into the games too. If a player is rewarded with new powers, weapons, or tools; these resources further empower them to be successful at the next level of the game. The added powers facilitate the intrinsic rewards of critical thinking practiced by the deep learner and they can be even more motivating to the player than the points, badges, and stars.

Perhaps one of the most important insights in the development of video games is that the penalty for failure must be manageable. In the early video games such as the *Super Mario Brothers* (Nintendo, 1985) a poor move could send the game back to the beginning. Players were conservative as taking a risk could lead to resetting the game. In more contemporary video games, the losses tend to be more manageable, a character is weakened or loses time, so that players can recover with some effort. Thus the players enjoy taking more risks and the environment is more comfortable. The video game designers have improved how they use the risk-taking principle.

When designing our classes and other educational experiences, do we think about the risks taken by the students? For many students, there is a significant risk of saying something in class that would be embarrassing. Yet, many class-wide discussions try to get students to offer ideas, opinions, or values. This is information reflecting the individual student and so there is personal exposure and potential for embarrassment. If students are forthright, honest, or provocative; the risks can be great. Even if the instructor is understanding and nonjudgmental, the students might not see it that way. Students are also prone to perceive something to be embarrassing when others do not recognize it as such. In relation to risks of speaking in class, the rewards for sharing meaningful perspectives are relatively small and the losses are imagined to be larger than they are. Class discussions become more superficial because the instructor has not managed the risk-taking principle. I am sure that most instructors realize this when conducting discussions; but they may underestimate how important it is to the students. Students are not learning as much if they are overly concerned with the risks of participating. If instructors are explicit about risks, it helps them develop ways for students to manage the risks. Different instructors have different ways of reassuring students, making them feel comfortable, and promoting a positive environment where risks are welcomed by the students as challenges. For class discussions, this can be done by having students discuss in small teams first, then having the teams report to the class, or having teams discuss the suggestions from other teams in a way that individuals are not connected to the ideas forwarded. The larger point is that instructors should be managing how students are acting in class, how they are taking or avoiding risks, as much or more as they are concerned with the content of the insights discussed.

Speaking in class is not the only place where students take risks. As mentioned, strategic learners wish to excel throughout. Anytime there is an examination, assignment, or activity that is graded, it involves risk. How can we structure our classes to get away from the risk adverse atmosphere of the early *Super Mario Brothers*? The contrarian would look at everything the students are doing in class and assess the challenges in relation to the risks. How can these activities be managed in relation to Vygotsky's (1978) zone of proximal development? Class assignments, projects, and expectations may have extrinsic rewards, but it should be as clear as possible to the students that they are working for the intrinsic rewards. That is how the instructor can lead students to deep learning.

THE GENERALIZATION PRINCIPLE

The idea of the generalization principle in video games is that when a skill is learned early in a game, it can continue to be used throughout the game (Shaffer et al., 2005). There can be many levels of such generalization. Initially the player picks up basic skills and later develops them through use in much more far-reaching and powerful skills. Players learn techniques to manipulate objects or objectives in the game that are then useful in a broader way at higher levels of the game. Just as with the reflective practitioner, the player needs to develop skills before using them. Then using the skills refines them and broadens their powers, at least if the player uses critical thinking to reflect on what is developing.

The generalization principle is closely related to the far transfer concept of Ambrose et al. (2010). The essence of education is taking a concept discovered in the context of a class and applying it to other classes, scholarship, or life in general. How often do we design our lectures, class activities, homework assignments, or examinations with the idea that far transfer is primarily what we are trying to achieve? To be fair, many class activities are concerned with the application of ideas presented in a class. Most often, instructors give examples directly related to the theory presented. This is near transfer, and the exercise minimizes how powerful the application of the theory can be. It is my belief that if we call attention to the generalization principle more often, we can do more than give the students examples of applications. We can be explicit in encouraging students to think of their own creative ways to apply the material. Yes, this does happen, just not enough. The point is that far transfer is the heart of a liberal education and thus it should be central in our course design.

THE IDENTITY PRINCIPLE

In many video games, the players identify with the characters they operate. They make choices within the context of the game from the point of view and values of the character. Gee (2007) has referred to this connection with characters as the identity principle of video games. Players can try out the different consequences of the decisions they make for their characters. The identify principle simulates real-life decisions about how to behave and how to develop ones character. Some games take the identify principle even further by defining different traits for different characters, including not just skills but values and emotions such as empathy, imagination, and judgment (Schell, 2008). Of course, exploring the world through other characters is not new with video games. Stories, books, and movies have long encouraged us to see the world from the point of view of characters from long ago, far away, and with values and beliefs distinct from our own. But in books and movies, those in the audience are passive observers of the characters. In video games, players can manipulate such characters and explore the consequences of their decisions (Gee, 2007). Thus, allowing the deep thinker to ask questions and test ideas as seen from the values and identities of others.

Being able to explore questions of identify, to see the world from another point of view, to understand motivations that are not our own, and to gain experience from acting on them; is an extremely valuable learning tool. An essential part of being an effective and powerful critical thinker is being able to put decisions in the context of another person's value preferences and world view. In education, we have used activities of role-playing, writing stories, and developing scripts to help students explore and ask their own questions about the cultures, values, beliefs, and sense of identity of others who are not like them. Yet, we have too seldom recognized this as an important component of critical thinking and effective scholarship. It should be integral in the organization of our classes so we can ensure that it is included in a student's liberal education.

UNDERSTANDING VIDEO GAMES

At this point, it should be clear that the discussion is not about the value of video games *per se*, but the insights they provide for motivating deep-learning behaviors. Video games, and games in general, provide examples of effective organization that motivates people to work hard, to stay on task for extended periods, to enjoy the process of learning, and to feel good about what they have accomplished. Video games are personally meaningful, experiential, and social. At their core, video games are based on reflective practice. As we try to design student experiences that promote more deep learning in our classes, we can certainly learn lessons by studying the design of video games.

There is a broad variety of completely different video games. Games come in all sorts. Different games employ different combinations of design principles and not all principles are included in all games. Many design principles forming the heart of some video games are not even considered in the representative list of six examples given above. This is parallel to the situation in education. There is a great range of different courses, instructors, and students. All with a variety of strengths and challenges. Just like with games, our learning experiences need to be designed with an idea about what is effective for the individual instructor, class, and student. Then our contrarian efforts at designing deep-learning experiences can be refined through reflective practice on an individual basis as student development continues.

Although video games, and games in general like the examples given in earlier chapters on jigsaw and crossword puzzles, have been used for comparison with learning; a further comparison can be made. Games reflect life. This is because games are primarily solving puzzles; games are meeting challenges; games can transport one to interesting places; games have competition and cooperation; games are all of the six design principles identified above, and many more that were not mentioned. Every profession has solving problems, meeting challenges, functioning in new environments, cooperating with others, and moving to the next level as essential aspects of skilled practice. Those characteristics are at the core of having an impact; they are more fundamental than knowing the ephemeral, yet rote, answers to contemporary questions. Even beyond our vocations, when we are living life in general; we are solving puzzles, meeting challenges, journeying to far-away places, dealing with the unexpected, cooperating with others, and competing with them too. A strong liberal education is preparing us to perform these essential life functions as well as we can.

Chapter 9

REFLECTIVE PRACTICE IN CLASS

THE INSTRUCTOR AS A REFLECTIVE PRACTITIONER

A Chinese proverb proclaims:

I hear and I forget
I see and I remember
I do and I understand

I like this proverb, but it is a little ambiguous. Is it is meant to imply that the sense of vision is better than the sense of hearing? Instead, I think it means that if I hear someone say something, like in a lecture, I probably won't remember it. The mental filing cabinet doesn't work well unless I have a structure to allow me to file the memory in a way that facilitates retrieval. If I see something, if I witness it directly, it seems more real and it makes a bigger impact. I am more likely to remember it as I have more structure to help file the memory for easy retrieval. In this regard, witnessing a lecture can have more influence than reading the same words. Lectures can be lively. Reading can be lively too, but it is also even easier to lose interest when reading than when both hearing and witnessing a talk. I propose a variation to the proverb:

I read and I fall asleep
I hear and I forget
I see and I remember
I do and I understand

This brings me to the main point of this proverb, the line: I do and I understand. This line connects directly to the ideas in preceding chapters about reflective practice. With the apprentice model, one is doing the activity. Reflection and problem-solving facilitates memory, transfer to specific uses, and far transfer of the principles to new circumstances. However, again, I think the proverb could go further. At present it has a focus on an understanding that falls short of questioning. The reflective practitioner will develop questions as she or he does the activity. The ideas will be probed and challenged as the reflective practitioner applies his or her critical thinking skills. I do and I understand is all about reflective practice. Here is a new version:

> I read and I fall asleep
> I hear and I forget
> I see and I remember
> I do and I question and understand

Interestingly, reflective practice is not just at the heart of learning, it is what instructors should be doing. When done well, it is reflective practice to plan a course, to plan a lecture, to give a lecture, to interact with and mentor students, and to evaluate a course. Not all reflective learners are acting as teachers, but to teach well one must be in the mode of a reflective practitioner. In fact, the act of teaching should force instructors to question assumptions and meanings, to distill points to their essentials, to apply concepts in new ways, and to express the material clearly and succinctly—an activity that refines and improves ideas and leads to new questions. It may be contrarian to think that teaching and learning are integrated, but I assert that teaching and assessing the students' learning and improving our own insights from teaching, is a high form of learning. Thus, the parable should be:

> I read and I fall asleep
> I hear and I forget
> I see and I remember
> I do and I question and understand
> I teach and I learn

Here is a related contrarian idea: If one wishes to learn, don't take a class, teach it. When done right the role of the teacher embodies all of the reflective practice ideals that the student role does, but it sharpens them even more. One becomes responsible not just for his or her own learning, but also the students' learning. The pressure is on the instructor to get everyone working together toward common deep-learning goals. Often choosing the learning goals and leading the way further enhances the learning done by the instructor. Most importantly, when an instructor is demonstrating reflective practice, it is a great model for the students. How often, though, do instructors make a point of demonstrating their own reflective practice to their classes?

SEMINARS

I have taught about every kind of class in the curriculum of a university. The introductory classes are my favorite classes. However, the seminar-format classes, either graduate or undergraduate, are also tremendously fulfilling to teach. In the typical seminar the instructor picks a topic, such as a specific line of research in a subarea of a discipline which is best if it relates to the professor's passions, and assigns journal articles to read in the area. The journal articles may be chosen with a purposeful sequence to develop a line of inquiry. The classes are limited to between five and ten students. Usually a different student will lead the discussion of each article. The students use their critical thinking skills to analyze the strengths and weaknesses of each article: How good is the evidence? Is there significant ambiguity? What are the unstated assumptions and are they reasonable? Does the evidence address the reasons and do the reasons connect directly to the theory? What does this mean for applying the underlying theory? What new studies should be done and why?

Although students are not put in groups and they are not moving around the classroom, in the seminar format the students are very much active participants. The discussions involve participation in learning. Instructors guide the seminar discussion, as such, they must be among the best critical thinkers in the class, but without stifling points of view that are not their own. An important contrarian position is that the purpose of the seminar is not to impart insight about any instructor's own research interests or values, but to get the students to improve their critical thinking skills and to model reflective practice about scholarship. When students teach each other in this way, they can inspire reflection and creativity. Students influence each other differently than the instructor influences them. The combination of an instructor directing critical thinking and students mentoring each other leads to powerful learning experiences. Further, students make the instructor think. I find seminars to be stimulating. Seminars continually help me illuminate my own points of view and give me ideas for future research. The reflective practice generated by the seminar format is a good example of why teaching enhances an instructor's learning and thus stimulates scholarship in a research university.

ACTIVE LEARNING IN CLASS

Colleges and universities have classes of many sizes. The seminar size fits the ideal of scholarly inquiry for reflective practice, but reflective practice can be fostered in classes with any number of students. How can we do this? That is, how can we use our classes to move students to more deep learning? For one thing, we can get students to appreciate the important roles of lectures, documentaries, and other one-directional media. Students should not just listen and take notes. They must use their critical thinking skills to evaluate the material and to develop their own questions while they are listening. Questions should flow directly from the student's critical thinking skills: What is the instructor's issue, what are the reasons, how good is the evidence, how does it connect to the reasons, and so on?

Further, beyond getting students to use more critical thinking in one-directional experiences like lectures, instructors can come up with activities that push students to perform as reflective practitioners in the classroom. This is called active learning. Developing ideas for doing this has been one of the most exciting and productive areas in the scholarship of teaching and learning over the past two decades. Many great books review the large range of course structures and class activities used to foster active learning (see for example, Barkley, 2010; Weimer, 2002; and Benassi, Overson, & Hakala, 2014). As these techniques are available elsewhere, I won't repeat them other than to note that the evidence clearly shows active learning can make a difference in student-learning outcomes. Freeman et al. (2014) performed a meta-analysis of 225 scholarly studies analyzing the efficacy of active learning. Their data show that active learning significantly boosts a number of performance measures across different areas of science, engineering, and mathematics.

What then should we do with large lecture classes when the students are generally taking a surface or strategic approach to learning? Even with the largest classes, one can divide the class into teams or groups and force the students to react with each other and to reflect on the topics of the class (Michaelson, Bauman-Knight, & Fink, 2003). Although this can be awkward when classes are to meet in large lecture halls, it can be done (Folkins, Friberg,

& Cesarini, 2015). Moreover, universities have been pushing to design interactive teaching spaces that will accommodate large numbers of students (Sawyer, 2013; Koper, 2014). Personally, I have been involved with students working in groups in the classroom for many years (Folkins, 2010). In my last five years of teaching, I would lecture on occasion as my ego demanded some pontificating, but I would use group activities to a large extent in every class period. The only exceptions were the small seminar classes that I noted in the preceding section.

A guest at a dinner party once threw out a challenge to me along the following lines:

> I hear your innovative teaching methods use groups of students. That is not innovative. I tried using group discussions years ago. They don't work. The students all resent that I am not talking and they are paying for a lecture. Further, the strong students do all the work and the weak students slide. This builds resentment in the strong students, who should instead be encouraged. In fact, one of the reasons group discussions don't work is that classroom discussions in general don't work. The students can't be expected to know enough about the material to have a meaningful discussion or to be leading themselves to correct answers. There is no good substitute for the professor talking and the students listening. That is what they are paying for.

I would agree with the guest in that what she was describing is not innovative. I would disagree with the assertion that discussions are not as good as lecturing. Class-wide discussions have long been a staple in the humanities classroom. What is important is how one uses groups and discussion. The pivotal issue for the contrarian is that the students are engaged in reflective practice that builds critical thinking, whether this is done in small groups, class-wide discussions, or even one-dimensional lectures. Reflective critical thinking is what will guide development of their own questions and lead them to deep learning. Too many group activities and class discussions do not build this sense of inquiry. Instead, they require narrowly defined actions that lead directly to correct answers. The instructor poses the questions, not the students, and she or he determines the only correct answer. The students realize this and they resent that the instructor didn't just give them the proclamation directly and not waste time on the activity. Remember in Chapter Four when the traditional science laboratory activity was criticized? This is the same issue. Traditional science laboratory activities tend to provide problems

that illustrate a basic theory the students have learned. Then the operation of
the theory is applied; that is, there is near transfer; and a specific correct
answer is worked out. Students do learn the application of the theory and how
to use the equipment. However, the overall activity is not much more
inspiring, and often less inspiring, than the lecture. The traditional laboratory
exercises were not designed to lead students to their own questions. They
don't foster deep learning.

The larger point is that traditional instruction; whether via lecture, group
activity in class, class-wide discussion, or a science laboratory project; tends to
follow the theory-first model of instruction rather than reflective practice. How
do we turn this around and develop students as reflective practitioners? The
simple answer is to use the intrinsic rewards of problem solving discussed
above when considering puzzles to build interest and foster a desire in the
students to ask their own questions. Students in deep-learning mode will tend
to do this automatically during a lecture. Students in strategic learning mode
won't. The other activities, especially group activities during class, can be
quite effective in generating the intrinsic rewards of problem solving and
leading to student-generated questions. Some of the ways to use group
discussions can help facilitate this, such as 1) doing group activities in class,
not having students work as a group outside of class and then providing a class
presentation with the answers they found[42], 2) keeping students in the same
groups all semester to build teamwork and competition among groups, and
most of all 3) structuring group activities around puzzle solving that not only
involves critical thinking, but opens up more questions than it answers.

What does one do in the team activities? One approach is to treat them
like a seminar. In a seminar students do readings outside of class and then
work as a team to interpret and apply them in the seminar. Instead of
discussing readings done outside of class, students can do many types of
activities that employ critical thinking and assess how well it is being done. In
active learning groups, the instructor typically needs to be much more
directive than with a team of graduate students; that is, one should: set up
explicit challenges and goals for the teams, keep activities short, have teams
report out often, and continually question the teams to get them to question
themselves.

---

[42] This is also useful as students often resent group activities when they are required to meet as a
group outside of class and it becomes difficult to find a meeting time.

As classes get larger, the instructor cannot get around to sample the discussions at very many teams. If a graduate assistant or two are not available, use peer facilitators. Peer facilitators are undergraduate students who have already taken the course. The peer facilitators attend classes, help monitor discussions, and act as a resource for students. Other students identify with the peer facilitators in age and experience and in some ways they may be more accessible than the instructor. Peer facilitators can often be a valuable resource to complement explanations offered by an instructor. Peer facilitators can sign up with the instructor for extra credit to compensate for this work and peer facilitators often learn a great deal from the experience making the credit well earned. The peer facilitators are acting as reflective practitioners.

It was mentioned above that keeping the same groups together all semester is important (Michaelson, Bauman-Knight, & Fink, 2003; Folkins, 2010). I found that this builds a great sense of teamwork and because of this I have referred to them as teams rather than as groups. Team members develop good friendships and the students report that they like this aspect of getting to know their peers much better than with lecture classes. I have even had students from the same team start dating each other. Students in a team go out of their way to support each other in class. As with the seminar format, students highly value the opinions of their peers and the learning they stimulate with each other complements learning directed by the instructor. Also, a great sense of competition will build between different teams through the course of the semester. The biggest complaint about the teams that I get is that students resent it when a team member misses a class. The remaining students feel disadvantaged and they pressure each other to attend. I like to compare this to an athletic team that plays together for a season. They build teamwork within the group and healthy competition with other teams helps to motivate and direct them. In many ways, this combination of collaboration and competition prepares the students for working in teams throughout their lives.

Following Michaelson et al. (2003), I use the following procedures to organize student groups:

- Call them teams, not groups. Be explicit in fostering teamwork within the teams and have activities that develop competition among teams.
- Many people, including students, will tell you not to keep the teams together all semester. They argue that students shouldn't get stuck with the same people all of the time and that they will learn more from a larger exposure to different people. Resist this temptation. As

with athletic teams, the teams bond and work together progressively well as they get to know one another better.

- Form the teams during class so the students see the teams are balanced. Don't put top students together on purpose. Don't separate top students on purpose. A good approach for selecting teams is to do it randomly, but one can mix students up by balancing majors, gender, or nontraditional versus traditional students.
- Assign as few as three students and as many as eight students to each team; although five-to-six students works best.

LECTURES

After Moses took the tablets with the Ten Commandments down the mountain, he talked to the collected followers. The ancient Greeks had great orators like Demosthenes. Kings and queens have addressed throngs of their subjects through the centuries, from Cleopatra to George VI. It is reasonable to conjecture that one person has been talking to groups of many people through the millennia going back to the origins of spoken language. One can call it an oration, a speech, a sermon, or a lecture. It doesn't matter. The practice of public speaking has been with us for a very long time. That is probably because it works. We are often moved and inspired when we hear somebody talk and make a good argument. The contrarian instructor would point out, however, that lectures work only to the extent that students are ready to listen and care—they need to be ready to not just listen, but actively apply their critical thinking skills and develop their own questions.

Some lecture environments are made to facilitate critical thinking in all of us. For example, when Moses came down from the mountain, although it was long ago and it is hard to know the thinking of the crowd below, a thoughtful person might have questions to ask about what the Ten Commandments really mean: Can I tell a lie or is the prohibition against all lies, even white lies, or lies done for a noble purpose? Can I kill to defend myself? How about capital punishment? What is really meant by coveting thy neighbor's spouse, how far can we go? The critical thinker will find significant ambiguity in the Ten Commandments. In situations like this, when the audience has reasons of their own to care and questions of their own to work out, lectures can work well. If the audience is there because they are required to be there and they do not see the relevance of the material for their lives, when they don't have their own questions and interpretations, then lectures often fall short of desired outcomes. In these cases, the content of the lecture doesn't matter much, it won't be fully understood or remembered for long.

Interestingly, for lectures the size of the group matters. If a speaker has a few listeners, fine. If more listeners are added, somehow the presentation seems to take on a little more importance. As the size of the group grows, the listener begins to imagine that there is something special about the presentation. It is a common inference, which is often false, that the value of the message can be judged by how many people are attracted and how many people are touched by it. In our society we tend to see a large arena or other gathering and infer that the popular speaker must have something to say. Politicians and preachers brag about the large crowds they attract. It is easy to mistakenly infer that this means their message is important.

This brings up a contrarian point. Small private liberal-arts universities, like the one I attended as an undergraduate, know that small classes can be a better learning environment than large classes. That is the case for discussion-based activities when the class is not divided into teams. I agree. In many respects one of the tremendous benefits of small liberal-arts universities is the personal contact from instructors. Yet, if almost all of a class is designed around lecture, then each listener gets the same lecture regardless of class size. If lectures with a large attendance are interpreted as more important than small ones, then big classes are positioned to have more effect on the students. Further, if students are grouped into very large lecture classes, then fewer lecturers are needed, and one can choose the presenters with the most talent and most engaging stage-presence. Large class sizes could be used to justify higher production costs for some activities or spending the time and effort to polish a top quality experience. The thrill of the experience at movies, theme parks, and video games is often facilitated by their high production costs. Thus, large lectures could be better than some smaller ones because one could spend a substantial amount of time, effort, and money refining them and making them a great experience for the audience. A caveat should be added though, that the polish and charm of the lecture is not what should be refined, instead the lecture should be examined and improved by looking at the questions it generates in the minds of those listening and thinking.

One can make the argument that in most classes of any size, lectures are not designed for student questions to be asked out loud, or at least, questions are primarily asked to clarify a point. When lecture classes are large, it is more likely that someone will ask the necessary clarifying questions. The value of a large lecture is not related to the lecturer-student interaction. Thus, the large size of the lecture audience does not detract from intimate interactions between student and teacher. There isn't much interaction anyway[43]. Hopefully, the deep learners are thinking about their own questions concerning the content of the lecture and making notes about where to look for answers to them.

When students are in large lecture courses, the student-instructor interaction comes from recitation or discussion sessions. These sessions are scheduled at different times from the lecture and they involve a teaching assistant or other instructor and a small group of students. Typically, new material is not presented in the discussion sessions. The object is to review, discuss, probe, and think critically about the material that was presented so eloquently and forcefully in the large lecture. While Associate Provost at the University of Iowa, I worked with the faculty members who taught in the University's largest classroom, McBride Hall auditorium. With a capacity of over 700 students, this auditorium was the location of many stimulating lectures. The faculty members giving the lectures would meet once a week with the 20 to 30 graduate-student teaching-assistants who led the discussion sessions for undergraduate students in the class. The students often reported that the classes in McBride Hall auditorium were among their favorites. The lectures made them think and the discussion sections allowed them to share questions and answers with others. Lecturing works and often the bigger the class, the better.

The contrarian concludes if one has a choice between a large lecture class and a small lecture class, it is often better to take the large one. There is a qualification in order. Remember reflective practice? The large lectures only work if the students are in a position to reflect on what they have heard. Are they in a deep learning mode to think critically about their own questions? What are the issues as the students see them? What are the reasons? What is the evidence? Are there logical fallacies in the argument? Can the students create applications and ask probing questions about the implications? If so, lectures are superb. The problem is not in the size of the lecture hall or the eloquence of the lecturer. The problem is that many students, especially in the first couple of years of college when these large lectures are most prevalent, do not have the tools to be skillful at critical thinking as described here. They listen to lectures in the surface or strategic modes rather than moving into deep learning.

---

[43] One could, of course, divide even the largest lecture hall into groups of students and the students could have discussions in their groups. I have a colleague who does this throughout all of her class meetings in lecture halls with as many as 250 students.

TECHNOLOGY: IT DOESN'T MATTER MUCH

The impact of technology on our world has been tremendous. That is the case over the last few centuries and the last few decades. Expectations have been great. Expectations have been exceeded. Hold on, it is likely to get better. Hooray, it is fantastic to be able to do so much more and to do it more easily and more inexpensively. With the digital revolution, every industry has changed significantly in how things are done and what can be done. Technological change has a ubiquitous reach. A few examples help to make the point: Think of the upheaval in the music recording industry. Think how special effects in the movies have changed. Think how the movie industry has morphed, along with television and videos of all sorts. Scheduling and controlling transportation is hard to remember, or even imagine, without digital technology. Communication is a fire hose and digitally-based social media. The list goes on. Technology is changing our daily activities in profound ways. In higher education, every academic discipline has powerful new tools and new insights that would not have been imagined just a few decades ago.

Many have thought that technology would also change the educational experience in profound ways. In 1913, Thomas Edison predicted that the movie projector would replace books (Freedman, 2003). When television came out many commentators assured the public that televisions would not only replace movie theaters, but also the teacher in the classroom. Then there were teaching machines, programmed textbooks, video-taped instruction, computers in the classroom, online education, flipped classrooms, and Massive Open Online Classes. Every one of these innovations was hyped as portending a complete transformation of college teaching. Many of these innovations have been beneficial, but there has been no technology-inspired revolution[44]. The contrarian would explain that changing everything doesn't matter much. At least, technology doesn't matter much for college teaching if one is thinking about how students go about deep learning (Stoll, 1999).

Let me give some personal background. I first learned to program in Fortran IV in 1971. Later, to analyze statistics for my doctoral dissertation, I had boxes of paper punch-cards that I carted across campus on a dolly. I have followed and used technology as a scientist and educator for decades. My children insist I am out of date and always will be. For twenty years I led

---

[44] Best (2006) provides an informative discussion of why people embrace the latest fad.

university efforts to put technology into classrooms. In the 1990s I was sure that if the university spent thousands of dollars to wire each seat in an auditorium, we could entice instructors to use clicker technology for immediate student responses during a lecture. I visited Apple in Cupertino and Gateway in Sioux City. I was an early participant with the National Learning Infrastructure Initiative which pioneered uses of learning management systems like BlackBoard or Canvas. I bought into the hype that was all around me. I remember a university regent in the 1990s insisting that with digital technology, online learning would be the norm, and accordingly we did not need to build new classrooms or rehabilitate the old ones. I listened to the remarkable accounts about Massive Open Online Courses[45]. I have watched the technology-based innovations improve higher education, and I am proud to have played a role in making today's technology to support student learning what it is.

Here is the rub. Student learning is a contact sport. One cannot just lay out information to students in a lecture or any other forum. If that had been viable in the past, parents would have purchased encyclopedias, made their children read them, the children would have become deep learners on their own, and colleges would have gone out of business decades ago. If that were the case today, we could replace the college experience by purchasing a computer and connecting to the web. Here is a quote from a recent blog by Annie Murphy Paul (2016):

> I often see people in the education world (especially the online education world) assuming that if information is made available to students, they will use it to teach themselves what they need to know. This assumption reflects a deeply flawed understanding of how learning happens among novices (and that's what children, and many adults, are). Learning is most effective and enjoyable when it is carefully sequenced and scaffolded.

Learning is a contact sport. Yes, the contact can be from a great instructor in a large lecture hall or in many of the others forms I have been reviewing. Now the contact can be effectively done online. I have taught seven online classes and love them. But the requirement for contact and how it works has

---

[45] Most of these tantalizing reports didn't mention the extremely high dropout rate from these classes. But then, if there are 10,000 students in a class, one still has a 1000 students after 90% drop out.

not changed with the technology. It won't change because it is part of our human nature. Technology can facilitate, but it cannot replace, a mentor's passion, guidance, and direction with the reflective practitioner learning to hunt on the prehistoric veld.

CONTENT ISSUES

Understanding the concept of deep learning has two aspects. The first is that deep learning is a style of learning where the individual pursues his or her own questions. The second is that it is also learning that is not superficial, but takes main ideas and drills down deeply to understand them. Then the deeper level of understanding can become a framework for more insights as the students encounter new ideas, attack them with their critical thinking skills, and use them as the basis of new ideas. Deep learning can be organized to provide the scaffolding mentioned by Annie Murphy Paul above which is fundamental to climbing upward within Vygotsky's zone of proximal development. If we have too much new content, we can't remember it all, if we can even remember much of it. If the content is broad, we spend our effort on a constant stream of new ideas and concepts and this tends to crowd out attempts to probe deeply. We need to stop and ask our own questions and analyze what we find; that is, to think critically. As Willingham (2009) explains, if we spend time to drill deeply into material, to analyze it, and to question it, we are much more likely to remember and use far transfer.

As instructors think about what is covered in our classes, it is important to review each unit or lecture, and to consider how all the components fit into the class as a whole. But the contrarian will point out that the most essential thing is not to be overly concerned with content, that is, what material is included and what has to be left out. Content may be somewhat important, but one should give primary attention to how the unit and the course are organized to foster deep learning. Where will the students be applying their critical thinking skills? What are their questions? How does critical thinking about one topic early in the lecture foster critical thinking about another topic considered later[46]? Has the necessary information been included and organized to guide that critical inquiry? Beyond that, are there topics or other material that can be omitted, thus allowing more opportunity for student reflection and deep

---

[46] This is the generalization principle from video games.

learning with the expectation that the deep learner can approach the omitted topics later in a more meaningful way?

These contrarian perspectives turn out to be difficult to put into practice. I can remember a discussion with a colleague once in which he mentioned he had over 150 PowerPoint slides for one of his lectures. I pointed out that he might have too many. His response was that he was lecturing to first-year medical students. People die from the disease that was the topic of this lecture and this one lecture would be some of the students' only exposure to the theory related to this disease in the curriculum. He insisted the topic was just too important to leave out any of the material. I argued, but I could not persuade him that more is not better and one can have too much of a good thing. As instructors, we all love and respect our discipline and we understand how important it is for others to know about all of it. Thus, we have an understandable tendency to include too much. The contrarian would point out that including too much content is probably one of the most common mistakes made by instructors. It is the enemy of student reflection and deep learning.

Once I was talking with a friend who was planning to be a minister. He said when thinking about his future career, he was concerned with coming up with a fresh new sermon every week. I pointed out that many religions, perhaps most religions, don't typically change anything in the service from week to week. Would people get bored? Not if they are comfortable with the routine. Repetition can be good. When people become comfortable with routine, it allows them a chance to think and to reflect. Parishioners can be behaving as reflective practitioners and learning from their own analysis of their lives through the guidance of their religion. The contrarian instructor might not necessarily wish to give the same lecture over and over, but a repetition and routine that sets the stage for student reflection without adding much new material can be very desirable.

Here is another example. When I was a Provost, I gave presentations and talks on a regular basis. At first, I went out of my way to mix it up. I assumed that it was important to make every presentation fresh and different, even when each audience consisted largely of new faces. I also searched hard for scholarly topics and this brought in themes from many places at many times in history. For example, if I gave a talk at the library I would find a way to touch on the evolution and progression of the American research library. I soon started paying attention to my feedback. What had others thought? It was clear that I had too much variety. I needed to find a theme or two and drive those themes in with every presentation. Maybe I might have approached the themes in different ways each time, but the audience wanted consistency. They wanted the comfort of knowing what to expect and then to connect their own critical thinking to the themes in a new way. If a presenter tries to have too much variety, or tries to make too many points, then the audience will not think deeply about them. The audience won't have the time to reflect. The presenter will not stir their passions and stimulate the desire to understand that is fundamental to deep learning.

When giving speeches as a Provost, I also learned, unless we are specifically dealing with history, it can be useful to keep the examples and points to the here-and-now. The long-ago and far-away have a certain charm and some mystery. They are the stuff of literature and movies. But, history and geography need to be mixed with the here-and-now so that people can see direct connections to their lives. The here-and-now is what makes the news interesting. Spicing things up with lessons from distant lands can be stimulating, but they should be interwoven with direct connections to the listener. Change and abstract visions of another world can both be useful, but we don't want too much of a good thing. Unfortunately, I have been to many, many presentations on campus through the years where the speaker tried to cover far too much material or who gave too little attention to connecting the material to the lives and values of the audience.

The points made for a lecture above also relate to the content of a class as a whole. It is a natural tendency for instructors to put in too many different topics in a course and to move away from the here-and-now to compelling, but far away examples. Instructors are intrigued by their material. They have passion for all of it, so they can't leave anything out of a course. With too much of a good thing, the main threads developed through the course can get lost. Students need to develop the tools of critical thinking. Repetition helps them consider the reasons and think about the evidence. It allows them to drill deeper. That is why this book intentionally includes a lot of repetition. Some topics, and some of the same examples, come up again and again.

With too many topics to cover in a course, the time and opportunities to provoke deep learning slip away. The processes to motivate creativity from the familiar are not cultivated. Content is provided that is a mile wide and only an inch deep. In my opinion, this tendency to include too much material in a course is the most common mistake made by instructors. It is more important to keep the amount of material small than to have a clear and powerful voice or a magnetic personality.

Instead of content related to specific subject matter, every course should ensure that it gives significant attention to the learning process. Is the instructor modelling reflective practice? Are the opportunities for critical thinking helping to refine those skills? Is there attention given to debunking myths about how student learning works? Is there a climate fostering deep learning rather than encouraging strategic learning in the quest for extrinsic rewards? Are students becoming deep learners on their own; that is, does the material provided lay an adequate foundation for them to search for answers to their own questions and pursue their new-found interest in the general topic? Such deep learning is what builds a student's passion for a content area. As we shall see in the chapter on leadership, one should also promote development of leadership skills throughout any course.

CURRICULAR ISSUES

In addition to our tendency to include too much content material in lectures, units of a course, or in a course as a whole; faculty committees also have a tendency to pack too much into the curriculum. I have been to many faculty meetings or curriculum committee discussions where someone had an idea for a new course. The advocates for the new course would make a cogent argument for the importance and relevance of the material. The advocates would be impassioned and persuasive in their claims for why the content *du jour* must be included in the curriculum. Usually though, the argument centered on why students must be exposed to the content material. The contrarian would point out that light coverage of material is not of much value. Just being exposed to material will not lead to students caring to do more deep learning on their own and to develop far transfer with the ideas embedded in the topic. Yet, if the curriculum is structured to foster deep learning, then enterprising deep learners will search out their own exposure to new content that they believe to be of value to learn. This then leads to understanding, far transfer, and a personal passion for the content area.

The problem is that the process for curricular change is not symmetrical. It is easier and more common to make an argument to add material than it is to reduce or eliminate a topic or subject area. One is much less likely to hear impassioned arguments for why a course must be omitted or at least not required. Traditional instructors care more about adding a course related to their special interests. They are concerned less about whether a course they don't care much about is required or not. As a result, the number of required courses and other curricular embellishments grows steadily. Sometimes the faculty does come up against practical limits. Curriculum committees reach compromises, but these often add to the complexities of the requirements without making significant reductions in the amount of required material. Overall, just as with lectures and courses, the curriculum tries to require too much material. The system favors and rewards strategic learning over deep learning. The curriculum is constructed to encourage the strategic learner to learn and follow every requirement. It is biased against the reflection and personal exploration of the deep learner. Further, the next chapter will explore a number of out-of-class opportunities to foster deep learning; such as internships, student research, and study abroad. These activities tend to foster deep learning. Yet, when the curriculum is bloated with a large number of required classes, often to be taken in a prescribed order, the opportunities for students asking their own questions are squeezed out.

Although traditional instructors want to include too much, the contrarian has another concern with the college curriculum. In contrast to traditional instructors; parents, trustees, lay persons, and the public-in-general don't care much about the breadth of material covered. As reviewed in the second chapter, parents and students are focused on the vocational aspects of the college experience. To these groups, the central purpose for going to college is to get entry into a more desirable profession. Understandably, students want the content of courses to be narrowly focused to that end. Material that stimulates deep learning, exercises critical thinking, and leads to a life of learning and purpose is dismissed as unimportant unless it is directly, and obviously, related to vocational specifics. It may even be resented as potentially challenging family values. The broader curriculum invites misunderstanding by the public and with that misunderstanding comes a desire to advocate for a more vocational focus in the college experience.

Politicians and civic leaders often have an even more directed take on narrowing the curriculum to connect directly to vocational specifics. Public expenditures on higher education are justified as investments in developing an educated workforce. Credentialed graduates are vital as business and industry need knowledgeable people to lead them. Further, graduates from the sciences and engineering invent new widgets. Business school graduates start new companies to sell the widgets. The new companies hire even more graduates and the economy grows. Governments fund universities because they want them to help business and industry make more money, employ more people, and pay the government more in taxes. The economy climbs upward. For example, in 1945, former MIT Provost and Presidential Advisor Vannevar Bush published *Science--The Endless Frontier*. It laid out the case for how investment in science would lead to economic development: Innovative high-tech research funded by the government would generate new applications that would either grow or attract new industries that would spur the economy. Calzonetti (2003) has dubbed this as the triple helix to characterize the intertwined connections between universities, industry, and the government.

Universities have long been supportive of the triple helix as they love the funding for basic research. But there is a problem. The subjects of the university curriculum are based on the idea of a liberal arts and sciences education promoting deep learning and a search for understanding of our world. Often, politicians don't get it. Many politicians want to stimulate the economy, but not pay for the most essential element of doing so, a liberal arts and sciences education. Further, politicians can be biased toward science and engineering as they misunderstand the value of the humanities and the social sciences in economic stimulation[47]. Even worse, often politicians try to direct universities away from basic scholarship and to channel universities into doing the kind of application-based research that industry should be funding. When politicians try to direct the curriculum and to impose their views on others, opportunities for creativity are squeezed out. Deep learning suffers. Politicians are trying to be cost effective, but their efforts have the opposite effect on the economy and society.

In defense of the politicians, universities have never been independent ivory towers. Research universities, especially, have always relied on funding from one source or another and funding will not come for long periods without justification to the funders. The contrarian professor believes that there is a middle ground. Universities can do both basic scholarship and be responsive to applied societal expectations. Further, in addition to pursuing scholarship, it is the duty of faculty members to educate the public on the value of scholarship in all disciplines regardless of its practical implications.

There is another complication from the efforts of politicians to invoke narrow vocational perspectives on the curricula of universities. Richard Florida (2000) and Blake Gumprecht (2008) have shown that spin-offs from high-technology university research are not the major impact of universities on the economy. The most influential impacts come from the ways that universities concentrate talented and industrious people in a community. These college-town communities value and foster high quality cultural, recreational, and lifestyle amenities. The richness of the communities attracts and supports new firms and industries, including those in the high-technology disciplines

---

[47] Even university administrators can have more affinity for applied technical areas that are favored by the public and may be imagined to lead to more lucrative careers for graduates. See Knight, Folkins, Hakel, and Kennell (2011).

favored by politicians, as well as the fine and performing arts. These industries contract to use university facilities like libraries, computers, and electron microscopes.

Florida (2000) goes on to explain that society should not be thinking of itself as basking in an information age, or a knowledge economy, but in a *creative economy*. One of the most important factors in economic development is to get creative people together in common locations. The fine and performing arts are central to this creative mix. Artists exemplify the concept of creative people and the works they produce make their environment more attractive and appealing. The creative people invent, develop, and build. They attract other creative people. They establish and expand businesses. The contrarian would point out that the factors that work to build a community of the type Richard Florida envisions also work on undergraduate students. As students work together and learn together; they build a community in which they influence each other. If the fine and creative arts are part of this mix, student communities build a foundation that encourages creativity and deep learning. One should not think of a college curriculum as designed to train students for the demands of a specific profession, but to stimulate creativity throughout the community.

INTRODUCTORY COURSES

Every discipline has a course that introduces students to their content areas. This is the case for the different majors in a university or college. Even disciplines without a major at that institution may be represented by an introductory course. Prospective majors take this course first. Students who are shopping for a major may take the introductory course to see if they connect with the discipline. Introductory courses not only confirm a prior intent to major for many students, they attract majors, and they lay the foundation for later coursework for those who continue in the discipline. For students in related areas, the introductory course may be the only exposure to that discipline that they receive. Often these courses are part of a series of general education requirements. Introductory courses tend to be taken by first-year students or sophomores, so they are formative courses for their educational programs. For all these reasons, introductory courses are among the most important courses at any institution (Folkins, 2010)[48].

The introductory courses are taught in a variety of formats. I have taught the introductory course in my discipline many times, beginning in 1978. I have taught it in a lecture hall with 150 students with breakout sessions, in a smaller lecture hall with 60 students, in an active-learning format with 35 students, and online. Although my introductory courses have varied in size, the introductory courses tend to be among the classes with the largest enrollments in most disciplines. Thus, they are even more important.

Here is the contrarian's concern. The vision behind a vast number of introductory courses is that they should be survey courses. The primary consideration in designing the course is that students are exposed to the broad surface and all the corners of the discipline. The thinking goes: Don't leave anything out as the nascent majors will need it to build their future and the nonmajors need to be exposed once in their lives to the joy of each academic nuance in the discipline. Different faculty members in any department may lobby to ensure their area of specialization is well represented. Thus, there is pressure to add more content and so with increasing breadth each topic gets reduced in depth. Again, the course becomes a mile wide and an inch deep. For example, I just pulled an introductory psychology textbook off my bookshelf (Gleitman, Gross, & Reisberg, 2011). The book is magnificent with flashy pictures, sidebars, and other reader-oriented elements. My concern is that the book is overpowering in its breath. This standard textbook is designed for one course yet it is 710 pages long[49] and this is followed by a list of about 3500 references. Who are the authors trying to impress, instructors who want to include everything or students who need to be inspired?[50] This approach

---

[48] The most experienced faculty members often choose to teach in their areas of scholarly focus. So although, the introductory courses are among the most important courses offered by any department, they are broader than the areas of focus for individual faculty members. Subsequently, they are often taught by the least senior and experienced faculty members. The contrarian would argue that we should attract our best teachers to the introductory courses, regardless of their level of seniority.

[49] The pages are high and wide with a small font. So each page is the equivalent of about four pages of traditional 8" by 11" 11-point font.

[50] This textbook does have a comprehensive review of issues related to student learning, including such topics as intrinsic and extrinsic feedback. Unfortunately, the market for psychology textbooks is driven by instructors with the traditional point of view that introductory courses should be comprehensive. They want a course that includes a bit of everything and this textbook tries to meet that desire. So to be successful, this psychology textbook is not allowed to practice what much of the past few decades of research on the psychology of student learning has taught us.

encourages not just strategic learning, but surface learning. No wonder students get bored. How detrimental is this to fostering deep learning?

There can be a different vision of introductory courses. Instead of trying to cover a lot of material, one can focus less on surveying the latest findings and more on introducing a discipline's scholarly processes of inquiry. Instructors can demonstrate how scholars in their discipline approach problems and then get students to work on similar problems. They can show the type of reflective practice and critical thinking unique to their area of scholarly inquiry. Instructors can give just enough disciplinary content to provide a foundation to stimulate students to formulate questions of their own. Then instructors can provide resources and direction to allow students to address those questions and to do it as reflective practitioners of the discipline. Even if a student initially has no interest in the course material, it can be like a jigsaw puzzle or a crossword puzzle, in that the thrill of problem solving is stimulating enough to provide intrinsic feedback. If the instructor shows passion, that passion can motivate student questions. The greatest achievement of an introductory course is not to survey material. It is to set the hook into the value system of the student. Do students now see how stimulating problem solving and critical thinking can be in this discipline? Do students have the tools to follow up and, not just answer their own questions, but to become energized by the new questions that emerge? Learning can be so much fun in any discipline. Introductory courses should be centered around bringing students into the community of leaners who gain joy from problem solving in the discipline.

TESTING: ASKING QUESTIONS ABOUT ASKING QUESTIONS

Many traditional instructors will give one or two examinations during a semester, plus the final. The examinations are typically objective or short-answer essay. When evaluating tests, traditional instructors tend to look at whether the test fairly represents the content areas of the course in the same way the content was presented in class. Traditional instructors might look at whether there is a good mix of students doing well on the test, and thus, by inference they assume that the course is pitched at the right level and that students are learning the material.

Tests provide the ultimate extrinsic rewards for the surface and strategic learner. Tests are central in how traditional instructors evaluate and think about students. Further, testing is becoming more and more important in our society. Tests are used for college entrance, job applications, and entry to many, many other professional opportunities. Test scores of many types are being used politically in an effort to judge college effectiveness (e. g. Arum & Roska, 2010)[51]. Because of this, there has been a great deal of psychological study of testing. Psychologists know what works and what doesn't and the way in which traditional approaches to testing fall short (Willingham, 2009). In spite of this, traditional instructors tend to keep on doing the things in their tests that they have always done. Although these instructors take a scholarly, critical-thinking approach to interpreting the material they cover in their courses, they do not take a scholarly approach to studying the design of their examinations. For example, contemporary learning management systems allow instructors to schedule examinations online, many traditional instructors do not do so. The reason given is that instructors want students to be in class so that students cannot cheat Is this the best option?

From a contrarian perspective, the most important role of testing is to encourage deep learning and to provide the intrinsic rewards to the students for engaging in deep learning. There are many different ways to design testing and student evaluation in general. A contrarian instructor might consider many of the options and then choose the ones that work for her or him. I have found the following approach works for me.

First, I do not waste valuable class time on examinations. The greatest value of a face-to-face class meeting is that it is personal opportunity for students to interact with the instructor and each other. Examinations are a solitary activity and students are not allowed to talk with each other. So have the tests out of class. I assign a day for all students in a class to take an examination. The students do so by logging onto the examination function in the classes' learning management system. Students can take the examination anytime during that day their schedule allows. Not only does this not waste class time, it allows me to give timed tests that are longer than a 50-minute class period. I typically use 75-minute to 90-minute tests. Students often appreciate having more time to think and organize and to demonstrate what they can do. Testing for 90 minutes is about the limit before many students fatigue, especially if the tests are so long that few students finish early.

---

[51] As one might have guessed, a contrarian professor would not think such attempts are well guided.

Further, by testing online, I can have examinations as often as every two weeks without interrupting in-class activities.

If given the opportunity, some students will cheat. As mentioned, this is why traditional instructors insist on giving examinations in class so that students can be watched. However, when students are together in a class they can peek at each other's answers when the instructor or proctor is not looking. Now that many classrooms have students sitting at tables for group activities, the opportunities to copy another student's answers are even greater. To me, this is one more reason not to have examinations during class-time. I do request that when students take open-book, open-notes tests online that they do not consult with others and ask them the answers. Some probably do cheat by asking other class members for answers. They may try to text Aunt Shelley or Uncle Jeffrey who are practitioners in the discipline of the class, but interrupting ones test to talk to somebody else does not work well. Timed, reflective-practice oriented tests make it difficult to ask experts as there is not enough time to explain the question, have the expert work through the problem, and then to discuss and explain it to the student. Students might write down the correct answers to choose for objective tests and share them online with other students. I have found that this does happen. Yet, it turns out that email and text messages are much more permanent than informal conversations or sneaking a peek at a score across the table. The electronic messages tend to show up later and students are likely to get caught. Many learning management systems now have ways to scramble the foils on an online examination, and this can be used as one more defense against students sharing answer sheets electronically. Another option is to require students to take their online examinations at an institution's testing center where they can be watched and email and text-messaging options can be turned off during the examination.

The second important point that guides my test design is that I do not use questions asking students to remember content or the material covered. Students are not expected to recall definitions or pull facts from their mental filling cabinets as a surface learner would wish to do. Instead, they must have already done enough deep learning to understand issues so that they can apply them to answer the questions on the test. Students are to apply the deep learning they have already done when studying for the test. Examinations are open-book, open-notes, and open to internet-searches. I can do this as the questions I ask cannot be looked up. Students must figure them out. I ask questions about processes, about relationships, about interactions in the material, and how to far-transfer concepts to solve new problems. Usually though there is not only one good answer. This can be frustrating to surface and strategic learners, but deep learners like to use critical thinking to evaluate the advantages of one answer over another and understand what factors reinforce this value over another option. An easy way to think about this is that tests are not about nouns; i.e., characteristics that exist concerning persons, places, or things. The questions revolve around verbs; i.e., what happens when one circumstance or another is created or when a concept students have studied is applied in new circumstances. Essentially, the tests are about forcing students to engage in reflective practice.

When a traditional instructor first begins to create test questions, it is easiest to just look for facts that a student must recall. The idea of a contrarian designing a test question tapping a student's understanding of process seems much more daunting. However, try it. It is not so difficult. One approach is to ask short-answer essay questions about the application of a process discussed in class to a new area. In grading the short-answer essays it is easy to recognize patterns of a few good ways to approach answering the question, some partial approaches, and some common misguided approaches or misunderstandings. Following this, the instructor can create foils in an objective-question format to be used the next time this question is included in an examination. Then it is no longer necessary to go through the effort to grade short-answer essays.

A third aspect of my contrarian approach to testing is the distribution of scores I obtain. When I began as an instructor, I remember doing an item analysis of each objective question. I wanted every question to differentiate between the abilities of the students. I soon learned that this was frustrating to students especially some of the students who were struggling to keep up. It was best to put in some questions that all students got correct. This didn't help me evaluate the students as strategic learners, but it did reinforce the struggling students and allow them to earn an extrinsic reward. Initially, I also thought that if I asked a lot of questions about content, and most students got these questions right, then I had done my job as a traditional instructor. I had shown that the students learned something. I seldom thought that there might be little far transfer of the material in my class to future classes and applications in the work and life of students later. As a contrarian, I now realize that asking content questions and having large numbers of students get high grades gives the wrong impression to me and to the students. Students should be led to understand, not that they have learned the material, but that they are just starting out on the adventure of deep learning in the content area. One way that I approach this is that my tests are always timed and they are designed so that students barely have enough time to finish. Setting up such a challenge frustrates the strategic learners who want to get every question right[52]. Yet, tests that reinforce the idea that there is never enough time to figure everything out send the right messages to the deep learners. Having a time limit also helps send the message to the students that, if they spend time trying to understand material prior to the examination, then they will be able to use the time during the examination effectively to solve the problems it presents. It is surprising to me that having students get only about half of the questions correct on an open-book, open-notes, open internet examination does not create a mutiny. They soon learn that there is a meaningful, deep learning challenge embedded in the examination. They learn to take pride in what they have accomplished in the examinations and to me this is a great way to get them to appreciate deep learning.

From a traditional perspective, examinations serve three primary purposes: 1) to motivate students to study, 2) to evaluate which students have learned the most, and 3) to provide extrinsic feedback to students and make them feel good about the time and effort they have devoted to the course. From a contrarian perspective, an even more important purpose emerges. The act of taking the examination is a great learning experience. Students are engaged in reflective practice. They are solving problems with a time limit, so they are learning to perform skills necessary to practice the discipline under pressure. Traditionally, instructors do not wish to take too much time away from instruction for testing students. I posit that examinations that involve reflective practice are some of the best learning experiences instructors can provide. One cannot have too many examinations.

---

[52] Strategic learners can become obsessed with getting every question right and acing every class. They realize that our society uses grades to rank students. A strategic learner might take great pride in getting 98 points on an examination and he or she might look down on the student with only 95 points. A strategic learner might take great pride in a 3.9 grade point average and look down on another student with only a 3.6. The difference in learning across such students is meaningless, yet as a society we use subtle distinctions to determine who gets into graduate or professional schools or who gets the best jobs. Although it was not on Thomas Jefferson's list of the purposes of college given in the second chapter, as a society one of our purposes for college is to evaluate students, to decide who are the most industrious strategic learners, and to privilege them—even if the substance of the distinctions means little.

Chapter 10

REFLECTIVE PRACTICE WITHOUT THE CLASS

When we think about student learning in college, it is reasonable to begin with the topics addressed in the preceding chapter: the courses, the content of the courses and the expectations, as well as the impact, of the curriculum. Yet, it is well documented that student learning benefits from many aspects of the college experience that go beyond specific classes (Kuh et al., 2005; Pascarella & Terenzini, 2005). Even for online classes, the college experience is about the opportunity for interacting with and learning from others. College, in any of its forms, is so much more than what happens in class. The college environment is designed to foster critical thinking and deep learning. The college environment is designed to make the instructors think and grow, so that their students can benefit from such growth. This chapter reviews many of the ways that the collegiate experience encourages reflective practice even outside of class.

REFLECTIVE GROUPS

The seminar represents the ideal reflective practice of scholarship. However, the seminar process embodies how scholars function and one doesn't need a formal credit-bearing class to create the seminar ethos that invites deep learning. For example, many academic departments, or subparts of departments, hold regular journal groups. Faculty members and students meet in the late afternoon or evening and discusses a recent journal article. All of the rules and expectations for reflective practice inherent in a seminar are there. However, a journal group meeting is not a class. It is just a group of scholars voluntarily getting together to follow the attraction of learning about one of the latest contributions to the literature. In fact, these journal groups can be better than a seminar because a variety of different faculty members are there and the students also represent different specialty areas. Students are not being graded and so there is less pressure for them to slip into strategic-learning mode. In these journal groups, disagreements resulting from contrasting perspectives and values are common. In the ideal, everyone gets to see critical thinking played out at its best. In reality, the discussion can get sidetracked, and usually does, but the members taking an informal leadership role are expected to bring it back to its scholarly ideals. Journal groups are not classes. No one gets grades. No one gets academic credit. Yet, they can be some of the best deep learning opportunities in a university.

It is also common for academic departments to have a regular proseminar in which one of the members of the department presents her or his latest research or research in progress to faculty members and students. These typically share many of the reflective practices noted above for journal groups. The proseminars can be a little more formal than the journal groups and sometimes that is a benefit. Even though there is a presentation format, different faculty members may get into heated discussions in these sessions. The faculty members take strong positions. They are engaged. They can often be passionate. Yet, generally the faculty members use critical thinking appropriately and effectively. *Ad hominin* attacks are rare and generally not accepted by the group. Just watching the faculty work in this environment is a meaningful example for the graduate students. I can remember times when I gave a talk at a departmental proseminar a week before I gave the same presentation at a national meeting. I knew I was well prepared for the probing of my colleagues from around the country and the world after making it through the rigors of examination by departmental pundits.

When I was a professor at the University of Iowa I started a group called The Motor Club. It was modelled on a similar group I had heard about at the University of Wisconsin called The Gas Club. The motor club was a group of faculty members and graduate students interested in neurological control of movement. My graduate students and I were interested in how the brain controls movements of the speech articulators; like the tongue, lips, soft palate, and jaw. There were faculty members from other departments interested in how the brain controls eye movements, facial expression, finger dexterity, locomotion, and other limb movements. About 20 scholars participated at various times. Once a month we would gather and one member of the group would share a research study on which he or she was working. The others would comment and critique. The group might come up with ways to improve the study or to address the same theoretical issues with a different experiment. The Motor Club was very much like a proseminar with one significant difference: The Motor Club represented many different departments from across the university: physiology, psychology, bioengineering, physical education, anatomy, and speech-language pathology[53]. The diversity added greatly to the richness of the discussions and the level of insight achieved by the members. Deep learning can be greatly enhanced when stimulated by others who have different ideas and backgrounds.

When I was Provost at Bowling Green State University we started a program of Faculty Learning Communities. The idea was that at the beginning of the fall semester we would start a series of different faculty discussion groups centered around a topic of interest. These were very much like the Motor Club at the University of Iowa, except that each Faculty Learning Community had a theme related to improved teaching and learning rather than something in the faculty members' academic disciplines. This program began over ten years ago and has dealt with many topics. The topics for the 2015-16 academic year were:

- Active Learning Using Digital Techniques
- Internationalizing our Practices and Perspectives
- Understanding Student Motivation and Attitudes to Enhance Learning in STEM
- Strategies for Teaching Students with Disabilities
- Integrating Sustainability Across the Classroom
- Scholarship of Teaching and Learning Spaces
- Online Learning: Theory and Practice
- Service Learning

For the 2016-17 academic year, the Faculty Learning Communities are:

- Contemplative Pedagogy: Creating Mindful Learning Environments

---

[53] Much of my own work is in acoustics, and, even though I started the Motor Club, acoustics was not represented. There probably could have been an acoustics club too, but the University of Iowa didn't have the combination of scholars to make that work at the time.

- The Critical Think Tank
- Understanding Student Motivation and Attitudes to Enhance Learning in STEM (year two)
- Creating Meaningful "Writing Intensive Experiences" across the Curriculum
- New Faculty Learning Community

Like The Motor Club, these learning communities benefited very much from the interdisciplinary representation of their members. Artists discuss scholarly content with physical scientists, librarians, and graduate students— all with different backgrounds, ideas, and creative solutions to offer. The Faculty Learning Communities are also unique and separate from the proseminars and Motor Club models in that the instructors are sharing ideas about their teaching. Years ago, faculty members would be very open about sharing their research results and discussing them with others, but teaching was seen as more private. Instructors didn't discuss teaching unless there was a problem. The revolution in the scholarship of teaching and learning begun by Boyer (1990) has been slowly changing this culture so that faculty members now actively seek opportunities to share, evaluate, and test ideas about improved student learning. The faculty learning communities described here are part of the benefits of this change. In fact, one of the faculty learning communities that I codirected for two years had as a primary focus the organization of university-wide events at which faculty members would share innovative teaching ideas with a much larger audience than those in a learning community.

There are models for learning communities outside of universities. For example, when he was 21 years old, Benjamin Franklin founded a small discussion group called the Junto (Isaacson, 2003). It met on a regular basis to discuss the topics of the day, philosophical insights into practical issues, and schemes to improve the city of Philadelphia or society at large. The discussion was to be freewheeling, but it was not a gossip group. The Junto members worked to ensure that focus came back to topics such as science, politics, the economy, and philosophical points like personal freedoms as balanced with the common good. This was not a college seminar, but it could have been. It was very similar to the journal groups and departmental proseminars discussed above. Franklin never had the opportunity for much formal schooling, but it is clear he learned a lot from the Junto that others might have learned in college.

There was no formal leader of the Junto, and members stepped in to lead a discussion as appropriate. Yet Benjamin Franklin did serve as a *de facto* leader and made sure that others were taking turns and that the discussion abided by principles he devised for productive learning. These principles were based on soft Socratic dialog. Franklin favored listening and questioning to open confrontation. As reviewed by Isaacson (2003. p 56-57), Franklin thought that one should avoid:

- Dominating the discussion, the concern was "Talking overmuch ... which never fails to excite resentment."
- Straying off task, and Franklin used as an example his own propensity for: "prattling, punning, and joking and which only made me acceptable to trifling company."
- Seeming uninterested, as Franklin thought it rude.
- Speaking too much about oneself, as this is also rude, if not unproductive.
- Prying for personal secrets, "an unpardonable rudeness."
- Telling pointless stories, which become even worse when long.
- Contradicting and disputing someone directly, as it is more powerful to ask questions, to probe their positions and slowly divulge ones contrarian position.
- Being critical to the point of excess, "it's like salt, a little of which in some cases gives relish, but if thrown on by handfuls spoils all."
- Spreading scandal, although allowances can be made for some lighthearted gossip, Poor Richard would make it fun.

Although Franklin developed these points at a young age, he used them throughout his life and even urged them on the Constitutional Convention. I think these points are a useful guide for leading and participating in college seminars, if not business meetings and social discussions of all sorts.

A few years ago I had the opportunity to join a group in the City of Bowling Green, Ohio, called The Seminar. I participated for about five years. It had been going for a decade or more before I joined. The Seminar was a community group and as far as I know I was only the second professor to join the group. Although we didn't realize it, The Seminar was similar to Franklin's Junto. We met once a week and used our critical thinking skills to address the larger questions of the day. Of course, we also drank beer, wine, or bourbon and the discussion would routinely get off track to sports, family life, or gossip. But the general idea was to push for loftier issues. To analyze our collective perspectives, to consider options, to purport unbaked solutions, to learn from each other, to foster critical thinking, and generally share in deep learning. We dealt with social justice, personal freedoms, the Bill of Rights, the Ten Commandments, and implications of the latest medical or scientific news. We asked ourselves: How could the world be improved?

The Bowling Green Seminar was primarily a group of people from the city, not the university. There was the retired editor of the town newspaper, the retired chief of police, and a number of people in leadership positions with the county's social services. After I joined, we added more professors, but the university representation was clearly in the minority. The name, The Seminar, came from the participants who started the group. Initially, they had no connection to the university and the name was meant to be facetious as the group had no structure other than getting together for a fun discussion. But it was a great learning experience, the intrinsic rewards were motivating, and the experience rivals any university seminar I have attended or taught in 40 years of doing so.

The Bowling Green Seminar was in some ways better than an academic seminar or journal group because of the diversity of personal experiences. After years of taking one position on one social or political issue or another, I ended up changing my view due to the Seminar discussions. The Seminar was enhanced by the different backgrounds of the participants. The Seminar had devout liberals and radical conservatives to spice up the political discussions. There were participants with passions for this or that and we knew who would take what position on some issues. That didn't change the substance of the discussion. The group could marshal excellent critical-thinking based arguments, and then rejoice in a lively and meaningful exchange of ideas.

In our society people often shy away from political discussions at social gatherings. Such discussions can be too contentious. Friends do not wish to challenge friends. Some group members solidify positions instead of listening; they invoke the confirmation bias and take the position: our people don't believe that fact. Franklin's rules are typically not followed in such social gatherings, so people shy away. The Bowling Green Seminar provided the venue to make the Junto-like exchange happen. Our society should find ways to do this more often, both in university settings and in our social communities as a whole. However, we can go further. A significant limitation to the Bowling Green Seminar, and Franklin's Junto had a similar limitation, was that there was still not enough diversity of background, experience, and world view. The group was made up of successful adults who had lived most of their lives in the United States. Alas, the lack of stimulation from others with different backgrounds, values, and ways of addressing issues is not unique to the Bowling Green Seminar. It is endemic in almost all of our societies. Addressing ways to foster communication across disparate groups continues to be one of the most important responsibilities of our university and college system, even though it is not listed in Jefferson's list of college purposes in Chapter Two.

Why is it that the informal sessions; be they journal groups, departmental proseminars, The Motor Club, Faculty Learning Communities, the Bowling Green Seminar, or Franklin's Junto; are such useful learning platforms? Are discussions at the bridge club, coffee shop, barber shop, or beauty parlor just as powerful? Well, maybe. It depends if the discussion is goal-directed and follows the principles of scholarly inquiry. Is it just the latest update of neighborhood happenings, local news, family events? Or is it a meaningful, goal-directed discussion? Is there diversity of opinion and a value system within the members that is freely expressed? The distinguishing characteristic of the academic seminar is that the professor takes responsibility for directing the discussion toward meaningful goals. In the journal group or other informal academic setting, different members take turns steering the discussion back to goal-directed inquiry. The critical thinking approach is fundamental to the process and there is little tolerance for *ad hominin* attacks, red herrings, or other logical fallacies. One cannot begin by asserting first principles and broad value assumptions not shared by the group without being challenged. That is what separates the scholarly discussion in the academic hallway or the seminar, be it formal or informal, from the typical discussion we find in social settings.

An interesting caveat is that business meetings may sometimes be good learning experiences, other times they are not. A dominating leader may begin a meeting with a directive that cannot be challenged because of that person's authoritarian stature. Group members take notes and ask questions for clarification—kind of like many traditional lecture classes. This may result in some learning, but not much. Other business meetings are very much like seminars. Although there is usually a leader, the group is free to think constructively about a problem and to work out tangible solutions. In this case the seminar-like business meetings are significant learning experiences. They accomplish a lot to forward the mission of the company too.

There is another aspect related to the make-up of any discussion group that is an essential to the learning environment. As noted; the broader the experiences, cultures, and ways of thinking of the members; the better. Group membership needs to include those with background and understanding of the issues being considered. The Bowling Green Seminar couldn't gain much insight about nuances of constitutional law or nuclear physics because none of the members had a deep enough understanding of those topics to steer the discussion in meaningful ways. It is the same with every group. Discussions in the university hallways with colleagues or the Faculty Learning Communities at Bowling Green State University can be scholarly, because the participants know their field. Fundamentally, we have professors because of their insights and backgrounds in the fields they teach. Content knowledge is essential. The point of this book though, is that knowledge of the scholarly material in any field is not enough. Professors can't just know their stuff, they need to connect with the learners and exude passion for their topics, both outside the classroom as well as in it, to further deep learning in the audience as well as to learn from the audience. Another somewhat contrarian point is that in a lot of contexts, one doesn't need a professor. If the Junto is organized well with enough background from the participants, the tide of conversation will raise all the thoughts. The process of reflective practice among participants is what leads to learning.

MENTORING: LEARNING ONE-ON-ONE

When I was a young professor at the University of Iowa, I had a colleague who would stop by my office periodically and ask: "John, what have you learned today?" Initially, I was slightly annoyed by this as I was busy doing something. However, I soon realized that this question often led to some great discussions. My colleague was a scholarly pundit who would take critical thinking to excess. Together we probed many promising ideas; looking for reasons and evidence for why something might or might not be a creative idea. We both had enough background in the scholarly topics of interest to steer the discussion in useful directions. In a similar manner, it was not unusual in that department to begin a discussion with a colleague in a hallway that would spark an insight. An hour later, two or three of us were still in the hallway enthusiastically planning an experiment to test the concept. Scientists usually have many more ideas for experiments than they have time and resources. Usually scientists never get around to doing the hallway experiments, but the activity is still a great learning experience. The hour in the hallway is not wasted time. I would argue that the creativity it sparks make it one of the most valuable activities of a professor. Unfortunately, there are often those in oversight roles for universities, especially politicians for state schools, who want to increase efficiency by forcing professors to codify and justify time spent on various tasks. The hallway discussions would look anemic in such an analysis. Well-meaning oversight and imposition of a narrowly structured system can often lead to a loss in creativity.

Let us get back to one-on-one mentoring. In a well-known paper, Benjamin Bloom (1984) discusses *The 2 Sigma Problem: The search for group instruction methods as effective as one-on-one tutoring*. The idea of Bloom's paper is that students learn more from one-on-one discussions with a tutor than from conventional lecture-based instruction. His experimental research shows that the difference is an increase of two standard deviations. Bloom's one-on-one mentoring is the classical vision of learning by sitting at one end of a log with Socrates sitting at the other end asking probing questions that force critical thinking. Socrates, and Franklin in his footsteps, leads one to create questions and want to test them. It may be presumptuous for me to assert it, but I think that the scholarly conversations I have had with other faculty members as described above are similar types of learning experiences. The essential task of the instructor is to lead students as they learn to probe for meaningful questions—and to ask those questions of others in the hallway outside the classroom or in the residence hall. I rejoice in the one-on-one exchange. Such exchanges can be created anywhere if we lay the foundation for opportunities and let them happen. It doesn't require an instructor if participants help lead. The other week I had an inspiring discussion with friends on an afternoon's 20-mile bike ride. Even the most informal discussions can be steered by informed participants to employ critical thinking. Such discussions can be quite stimulating if they engender deep learning.

Significant evidence shows that students' one-on-one involvement with instructors outside of class will make a substantial difference in their education (Kuh et al., 1991). Apparently this does not happen enough, as Kuh et al. note that three-fifths of first-year students report they have "never discussed ideas from readings or classes with faculty members outside of class" (see also Selingo, 2013). Students should make an effort to seek out instructors and instructors should make an effort to make sure students know they are available and interested in meeting with them. Contact in class should set up more contact after class. Instructors can try to ensure that there are meeting spaces outside of class so discussions can be continued (Folkins, Friberg, & Cesarini, 2015). For example, when instructors connect theoretical material to real world applications, they might encourage students to not just develop their own applications, but to discuss these both inside and outside of class.

Too often students only visit an instructor's office hours when there is a problem. More typically, students don't even come to office hours when they have a problem. Traditional instructors often resent this, but seldom do much about it. Rather than sitting alone and working on projects they would be doing if it were not for office hours, why can't instructors take responsibility for attracting students? Instructors can't just mention that they are available if students have a problem. One-on-one time with an instructor is a valuable resource. If the students waste it, then the instructors are to blame for not inspiring them enough to want it and to learn how to us it. When students do show at office hours, instructors need to use the meetings, not to address the mechanics of assignments, but to play Socrates: questioning, probing, prodding, and moving the student to more directed critical thinking. Instructors can and should use these opportunities to get students to want to ask their own questions. If instructors do that, there will be the intrinsic reinforcements of deep learning. Students will realize their new powers, which will keep them coming back.

Kuh et al. (2005) explain that institutions differ greatly in the culture and approaches they have in making time for students as well as offering students more out-of-class learning opportunities. Such out-of-class activities can be extremely meaningful especially when instructors and other student-services mentors are involved directly. Those who study student life have produced a sizable literature on the positive effects of the residential college experience, as well as out of class programming for commuter students. It is clear that the many different organizations provide effective learning experiences, and these range from orientation sessions, Greek life, residence hall programming, attending theatre performances, attending music concerts, leadership academies, clubs, special events of all sorts like invited lectures or panel discussions, and the spectrum of team sports. Sports that incorporate significant learning experiences are not just intercollegiate athletics, but intramurals and club sports like fencing teams, chess teams, and forensics teams. It is difficult to measure the extent to which out-of-class experiences affect student learning, but it is clear that the effects are substantial and that one-on-one experiences with insightful mentors are among the most powerful of those (Kuh et al, 1991; Selingo, 2013).

It is interesting to note that although Kuh et al. (2005) identified a number of institutional characteristics and cultural aspects that promote student learning, the factor that was shared across the most institutions was a positive attitude about student success. Whether or not these institutions did anything that was specific and measurable, the faculty and staff members thought their institution mentored students well. This belief was the most important factor in student success. Faculty and staff members at these institutions also believed they could do even better in the future. They had confidence in their abilities and confidence can be an important influence in setting the groundwork for success (Kanter, 2004).

Remember the example given above about professors learning from each other through hallway discussions. Peers learn especially well from each other. We can make each other think. The traditional academic approach is that students learn from instructors in lectures and students learn even more when working with the most distinguished professors one-on-one. The contrarian will point out that students can and should learn as much or more from other students[54]. Learning is a personal activity of posing questions and seeking answers. Students need to bounce their ideas off their peers. There are only a few instructors for every student. Other students are easier to find. A student can ask the same question of many other students where she or he can only ask the same question of an instructor a few times before it gets old, or at least impractical. Perhaps more importantly, students do not have the same personal experiences as their instructors have had. Students connect to each other in age and cultural values, as well as in their level of development and experience. I would assert that it is good for instructors to be very different from students in these characteristics, but the students also need to be able to vet their ideas and seek inspiration from other students who are more like them.

STUDENT RESEARCH

It is common for undergraduate students to have the opportunity to be involved in research. This is a particular strength of the research university, but there can be a surprising number of opportunities for undergraduate student research even in colleges not directly engaged in research as part of their mission. There is a national association, the Council on Undergraduate Research, charged with fostering and communicating undergraduate research.

---

[54] Parents will often assert the same thing. That is, their college-age children spend a great deal of time talking with others their age and learning from them. Youth identify with each other and give a different consideration to information that comes from adults and from other youth. Although teenagers might not admit it, they continue to learn from their parents and other adults. It is just that older children thrive on the opinions and values of their peers. This is quite analogous to the academic situation. The input from instructors is valued differently from the input from other students. Both can be important and complementary.

Further, a significant amount of evidence shows the benefits of research experiences for undergraduates with many different majors (Kardash, 2000; Elgren & Hensel, 2006; Russell, Hancock, & McCullough, 2007). Such students have better understanding of course material, better far transfer, and more proclivity for deep learning. They also establish positive relationships with their research mentors. They develop passions for content areas. These students are more likely to consider careers involving research. Undergraduate research is clearly a good thing.

Typically, undergraduate research is undertaken in the senior year and takes the form of an honors thesis. Some top students elect to go this route. The research looks great on student resumes and strategic learners are attracted by the extrinsic rewards. Aspiring students meet with a mentor and find a research project. Often, a mentor will give a student a project that is a piece of a larger research program. Sometimes the student will come up with his or her own project. This is rare, and it can often be frustrating. Indeed, for most students finding the project to study initially is one of the most challenging aspects of the work.[55] One of the formidable complications with finding the perfect project is that there is significant time pressure. In many institutions the entire honors project has to be done in a year or less.

The honors thesis has many steps. After deciding on an experimental question to study, the students find and integrate the scholarly papers bearing on their topic. They learn laboratory procedures or other aspects of how to conduct the study. The students write a prospectus. This is approved. The students then submit the project to a human subjects review board, institutional animal care and use committee, or other oversight body. The approval process can take weeks or more. Then the students find subjects, conduct the study, measure the data, analyze the data, and write a paper. The entire process can be exhilarating and rewarding when it all works. I have mentored a number of undergraduate research projects and a couple even resulted in published articles in top-tier peer-reviewed journals. It is clear that individual honors projects can be a splendid experience in deep learning. However, the contrarian, as a critical thinker, might propose a bit of caution in interpreting the research showing the benefit of doing an honors thesis. Only the top

---

[55] I can remember when I was beginning in science. I thought that the most daunting challenge for any researcher was to come up with an experiment that hadn't been done before. Not so. Researchers usually have a list of research projects that they would like to do. The challenge is to prioritize the projects, pay for them, and manage time and laboratory resources. It is easy to try to do too much.

honors program students participate, thus the sample of students is based on the most interested of the best strategic learners in the university. Even then, some drop out as things go wrong. Consequently, the studies showing the benefits of traditional honors theses are based on a biased sample. These very dedicated strategic learners will look good, and better than other students, even without doing an honors thesis. How do we know that the honors thesis produced the purported gains when there is no comparable group with which to compare them?

The contrarian would point out that one must be careful advocating for honors theses for another reason. Even for small projects, the honors thesis is a tremendous amount of work for a student to do in one academic year on top of all of the other demands on college seniors. Many things can go wrong with the project that are out of the control of the student. Delays can be devastating if the problems threaten to postpone graduation. If the honors thesis project creates frustration, it can turn students off to scholarship. As a critical thinker, one might be asking: Are there better ways? Friberg, Folkins, & Visconti (2013) show that there are.

Attempting to do one complete study, from finding the topic through writing a formal paper, is asking a lot. Only the top students are attracted. Only the top students can get through. It is a demanding curricular design, if not a poor one. It seems more reasonable to have most students do only a portion of a study. Students could still participate in faculty-driven projects; they just don't need to be responsible for a complete study. Some students could do a literature review that turns out to be a useful resource to the researchers leading the study. Others could learn about data gathering, data analysis, or other laboratory techniques. When students are involved in running subjects or measuring data, they learn. Seasoned researchers may look at tasks such as measuring data or running subjects as tedious, but sometimes students new to the research environment look at this as a way to be included and to make a positive contribution. It is an initial stage in the process of reflective practice.

Sometimes different projects can be assigned to individual students. Other times groups of students might work on a project together. Students tend to hate group projects as required by traditional teaching methods. The students claim that others do not do their share or are not available at necessary times. I have found that this is the case for class-related projects assigned to be done out of class. It is very different if one gets sophomores or juniors introduced into a laboratory group. Regular laboratory meetings can be put on the student schedule. The younger students don't speak up much at first, but as they get more comfortable, they participate. Slowly the new students make friends with the older students. The more senior students mentor the newer students[56]. Again, students learning from each other is a valuable complement to their learning from instructors. Other students are a tremendous resource, if used well and if students use them to foster critical thinking and deep learning. What students learn from such interpersonal activities is also expected to facilitate far transfer. When students graduate they are mature critical thinkers ready to continue to learn from peers in their professions as well as other aspects of their lives.

Another viable alternative to the traditional honors thesis does not get much attention: Students can replicate a research project. Some traditional instructors argue that replicating a project is not original research. There is a point to that[57]. The Council on Undergraduate Research does not recognize replication as creative research and they do not support it for honors theses. The contrarian instructor may disagree. Most honors theses do not lead to publication and so creating original research is not necessarily that important. There are advantages to having different students do the same study. The students are not sidetracked by the frustrating need to find an original project that is doable in the time available. It is much easier for them to get a copy of an existing article and to test the same question. There are many other joys to doing research than deciding on the experimental question to explore, especially when students are not prepared to do so. It is not necessarily the case that students will be more interested in doing the research if they pick their own topic. Student interest in practicing an activity is not as influenced by an initial interest in the topic as it is by how meaningful the puzzle-solving skills are when doing the project.

If an instructor assigns a project, more attention can be given to the students' experiences in designing and executing the project. Students might follow similar experimental procedures used in the study to test or modify them in thoughtful ways. When many students replicate the same project, instructors become familiar with the study and the problems the students might encounter. Laboratory equipment or other experimental procedures can be set

---

[56] This is analogous to the way a 19th century one-room school house would work. The teacher can't be everywhere with everyone, as a consequence the older students teach the younger ones. Yet the older students also benefit greatly from the teaching process as it makes them remember, analyze, and explain what they have learned before. The process is not directly akin to reflective practice, but there are elements of it. Clearly the older students were better at far transfer after teaching the younger students.

[57] One could also argue that replication is necessary and useful in science.

up and used over and over. The students learn from carrying out the procedures and it doesn't matter much to them that others have done the same thing before. In fact, if studies to be replicated are designed well, students can learn a great deal from comparing notes and ideas with each other and using critical thinking skills to evaluate the findings. With replicated studies, it can be easier for instructors to give students feedback, as they know what to look for.

It should be emphasized that such replicated projects are fundamentally different from the typical laboratory assignments one encounters weekly in undergraduate science courses. Students are not following a formula and getting prescribed answers that demonstrate a well-known point about science. In the replicated studies described here, students are involved in developing creative research designs. Their findings cannot be judged as right or wrong. The studies are as usually as messy to interpret as the research they replicate.

In my last year of teaching, I tried a variation on the replication-study approach described above. Rather than waiting until students were majors and involved in a research laboratory group, I gave a reflective-practice project to a group of nine first-year, first-semester students who were in an honors section of my much larger Introduction to Communication Disorders class. All nine students were given the same research project. They were to use free applications on smart phones or tablets to measure the listening environment in classrooms around campus given tools described by Folkins, Friberg, & Cesarini (2015). The students had direction about the general question to ask, but they were to choose their own independent variables to support that larger question. Each student was to do her own work, to make her own measurements, and to write up the results independently; yet the students were encouraged to collaborate. I had break-out discussions during the regular class periods to allow students the opportunity to discuss their projects with each other. I was available for help, guidance, and even explaining how to do anything the students asked about. Although there were nine students, the assignment was not too much work for me as the students were all doing the same project. On my part, it was much less expenditure of time and effort than guiding a single honors thesis project.

Although all of the students attempted to answer the same general question, and they collaborated with each other, the projects produced were very different from student-to-student. The students had little background or theoretical knowledge about research design, acoustic analysis, or writing scientific papers. The papers showed their lack of experience and understanding. To me, the most interesting thing was that the students did not recognize how poor their papers were. They seemed encouraged in that they had been asking their own questions about how to do the project and finding their own answers. Collaboration with each other had given them support, but they were all independent enough to do their own work. The students had not been discouraged by the factors that come into play in an honors thesis, like finding one's own topic, uncontrolled time delays, or expecting that the study would be adding to the pool of meaningful scientific research.

Afterward, I had the students reflect on their experience. They were thoughtful and creative. One of the students disliked the project and dropped out. Six of the eight remaining students loved the project. They now thought research was of interest to them. The six students said they wanted to consider doing more research. They were already developing their own questions about acoustic measurements of classrooms that they might wish to pursue sometime later in the future. On their own, as deep learners, they sought out answers to questions they had about acoustic theory and experimental design. Note that initially the students were not interested in the general question of this study. But when they undertook the project, they were expected to act like reflective practitioners. The students developed their own questions about different approaches to conducting the study. The assignment became like a puzzle to them and they enjoyed the problem-solving. Due to the students' lack of experience, the final projects suffered from significant flaws in development, design, and execution. Yet, although the quality of the final written papers left a great deal to be desired, the students were using reflective practice to hone their critical thinking skills. They received significant intrinsic reinforcement from the activity. The intrinsic reinforcement may have been much more impactful on the students than the value of anything specific they learned. This project further demonstrated to me that even first-year undergraduate students can easily be reflective practitioners when given the chance, direction, and motivation.

One more point should be made about undergraduate research. Often one finds courses designed to introduce undergraduates to research. Some of these courses are designed to help students find research projects or research mentors. These are fine classes and I taught one for about fifteen years. However, in some of these courses instructors try to cover a lot of theory about how to conduct research. It can be intimidating if there is too much theory. Students are not only overwhelmed; they do not have enough experience with research practice to ask their own questions about experimental protocol. For example, I believe that one should not teach statistics at this level. The students can get statistical advice when they need it and develop expertise in experimental design in graduate school if they go that route. Teaching statistics and experimental design in these introduction to research courses is the theory-first approach eschewed by those advocating reflective practice. It has two drawbacks: 1) It doesn't work. That is, the students are still not able to design an experiment effectively. They need help either way. 2) It makes things worse. If students do not begin with the attraction of problem-solving, yet they confront the chore of working through the mechanics of the experimental protocol and statistical theory, they can get dyspeptic impressions about what makes scholarship exciting and intrinsically rewarding.

INTERNSHIPS, CLINICAL ACTIVITIES, AND ENGAGEMENT

Universities have been offering internships for decades. Academic programs make arrangements for students in their department to get experience working in business and industry placements connected to the major. These activities have been quite productive in connecting academic units to off-campus resources and they have also benefitted the businesses involved greatly. Internships are seen as quite desirable by both students and their parents, because it is well established that successful interns often continue with employment post-graduation. Yet, for all of the benefits of internships, the primary benefit is sometimes overlooked. Interns get to follow the apprentice model. Interns are put in the classic position of a reflective practitioner. Unlike with the traditional theory-first model of lecture-centric education, student interns have practical experiences that can lead to development of their own questions and direct their interest to the theory-intense courses they take later in the curriculum. Theory-intense courses will mean more to the students who already have questions the theories will help answer.

Since the time of the Merrill Act in 1863 that established our system of land-grant universities, it has been recognized that universities should be serving their communities with outreach programs of all sorts. Outreach includes a range of professional areas: health care and hospitals, legal services, agriculture extension services, home economics programs, business connections[58], engineering services, social outreach, support for criminal justice, and a long list of other areas. Since the Merrill Act it has been recognized that, not only should universities be involved in outreach, but that undergraduates should participate as well. In contrast to the traditional theory-first academic approach, and with the encouragement of academic contrarians, interest in engaged learning has surged over the past two decades. For example, the Carnegie Classification of Institutions of Higher Education now has a classification for Elective Community Engagement. The principle rationale is that students gain greatly from their personal experiences in learning to serve the community. Educational experiences should stimulate a student's social consciousness and connection to the community. I agree. Yet, the contrarian would argue that discussions about the value of outreach programs can sometimes miss the primary point. Connection to the community is great, but the most powerful benefit of these activities is that students are learning as reflective practitioners. As a consequence of their reflective practice, the students are more motivated to function as deep learners in the areas in which they are exposed. These students develop their own questions. They use critical thinking skills to solve puzzles and that leads to intrinsic reinforcement. Students can develop passion for the aspirations that drive the community in which they are engaged. They develop a life's work from the perspective of a liberal arts education, not from the perspective of going to college to get a better job[59].

It has been a long tradition in American higher education to offer a few students the chance to study abroad for a semester. I love these programs. About 45 years ago, I went on a semester long[60]program in Austria. Through the years, I have continued to build on ideas and values that I developed

---

[58] Outreach from universities to business is not just connecting the university to local businesses with students doing internships. There are many connections in technology transfer that include the process of patenting, copyright, and scholarly know-how. Technology transfer stimulates partnerships between higher education and industry, entrepreneurship, and the development of start-up companies.

[59] Some of the students might have been attracted initially by prior beliefs in these areas, but even these students will benefit from reflective practice, deep learning, and critical thinking. These experiences make the intrinsic rewards of such service more salient.

[60] Over the past few years many off-campus study programs have begun to be offered for less than a semester. For example, it can be great when students go to London to study architecture for the two weeks between the end of spring semester and the beginning of the summer. There are many other examples of new study and travel packages. Although international travel is becoming less and less expensive, some students are still challenged by the cost of foreign travel. The National Student Exchange allows students to study for a short time at different universities across the United States at a minimal cost to them.

during that program. Even though we are often poor judges of our own learning, I know that my semester-abroad experience was inspirational to much of my later development both personally and professionally. What is it about study-abroad experiences that makes them so beneficial? Even if formal classes are included, the overall experience is not much like the typical lecture course. Students are able to interact in new ways with history, art, music, geography, business, the list goes on. Students are immersed in a new culture that includes new customs, new social norms, and different values. Students are not just hearing a lecture about these practices, they are experiencing them. Students abroad have many problems to solve, and often they must solve those problems in a language that is not their own in a society in which the unstated value preferences and assumptions must be discovered. Although study-abroad programs are part of the traditional fabric of the university experience, they fit the contrarian perspectives explained here. Students are functioning very much like reflective practitioners.

International travel is now more affordable and more common than ever. Over the last four decades, countries around the globe have dramatically increased the number of students sent abroad (Sood, 2012). In contrast, in the United States, many universities are struggling to get students to go abroad in large numbers (Peligiri, 2012). Although many factors may contribute to the lower popularity of study abroad here, Peligiri (2012) raises the concern that students are now more vocationally focused and see international experiences as less related to training for their profession. It is also likely that the expansion in undergraduate curricular requirements is a factor. Students in many majors, especially education and nursing[61], are impeded from studying abroad because in these majors there are a number of required courses that must be taken in a prescribed sequence. Students can only go abroad if they extend their undergraduate programs for a semester, and even then a semester absence can sometimes put them out of the required course sequence and delay graduation an entire year. This is another example of how the well-intended desire to pack more content into student programs inadvertently results in less reflective practice and thus less deep learning.

---

[61] Although the curricula of these programs are tightly prescribed and sequenced by credentialing and accrediting groups, a few university programs have overcome the unintended obstacles created by well-meaning oversight groups. They have continued and expanded the incorporation of study abroad opportunities in their curriculum. Some of the majors in the College of Education and Human Development at Bowling Green State University are great examples of what can be done.

Chapter 11

STYLE MATTERS

    Throughout our lives, we care about how things around us look, sound, and feel. What are the images being sent in our culture about the way we talk, the clothes we wear, the car we drive, the home in which we live? We often make initial judgments of people, places, things, and experiences based on their pleasing design or the different types of symbols or meanings they have in our society. Universities and colleges have long understood and acted on this issue in the design of their campuses and traditions. For example, one can often be influenced by the character of a traditional residential campus with its ivy-covered walls and sandstone crenellations. A university campus can seem somehow set apart from other venues and one can infer that the campus must be a special place for learning. Commencements are another example of academic style. One can get caught up in the atmosphere created by academic regalia and the pomp that comes with music and character of the commencement event[62].

    How instructors dress also influences the style of the university experience. Centuries ago, professors all wore a cap and gown to class. I expect it helped create an academic tone although one might also note that the doctoral hoods were designed to keep the head warm and ostensibly later became a pouch to store materials in a pocketless robe[63]. Today, academics are free to dress as they wish, yet the contrarian might point out that they often

---

[62] One should note that the delight of the event can wear thin as the long, long, long line of graduates commences across the stage.

[63] I have thought I should show up at commencement sometime with a baguette and a hunk of cheese tucked in my academic hood in case it got to be lunch time.

dress the part of a scholar, with or without realizing it. Given that professors are well-paid and distinguished professionals; they do not typically dress like many other professionals. A professor in a business suit would look out of place and this is usually the case even in a college of business[64]. Professors dress in a very casual way[65]. This way of dressing sends a message to students and colleagues in today's world that academia takes pride in having its own distinctive style and character.

Clothing styles are an example of a much larger issue related to the character of academia. For example, academic materials, like scholarly journals, often are distinctly different from materials supporting other professions. Scholarly journals have strict requirements in terms of layout and presentation. Pictures, colors, and other materials were traditionally not allowed as they were too expensive and impractical to print. This may be slowly changing with new digital production methods. However, the academic style also focuses on the power of the written and spoken word. Colors and pictures are eschewed as fluff that distracts from the content. In spite of what technology can now offer inexpensively, it is our heritage for scholarly works to be clean, not sotted by distracting baroque embellishments.

Although clothing and scholarly journals provide examples of academic style, they are not really that important to students. What students care about much more is the tone and character of their learning experiences. There is probably nothing more evident to students than the style shown by their professors. What impressions do instructors have on students? It is not their clothes. Perhaps it is more pertinent here is to consider what teaching styles make the strongest impressions on students. Daniel Willingham provides an interesting discussion of teachers with impactful teaching styles[66] and he has identified four teaching styles thought to be most influential:

- Teacher A is the comedian. She tells jokes frequently. She never misses an opportunity to use a silly example.

---

[64] I might point out that this generalization does not apply to university administrators, even the ones who are also academics. For seventeen years I wore a business suit almost every day as a university administrator.

[65] Of course, there are a number of exceptions. Professors in a medical school dress like the physicians they are. In my own discipline, speech and hearing clinics have strict dress codes for clinical activities. These students need to look and act professionally as clinicians.

[66] I should note that Willingham (2009) was referring to the styles of K-12 teachers and not college instructors, but I think the generalizations still fit.

- Teacher B is the den mother. She is very caring, very directive, and almost patronizing. But so warm that she gets away with it. Students call her "Mom" behind her back.
- Teacher C is the storyteller. He illustrates almost everything with a story from his life. Class is slow paced and low key, and he is personally quiet and unassuming.
- Teacher D is the showman. If he could set off fireworks inside, he would do it. The material he teaches does not lend itself easily to demonstrations, but he puts a good deal of time and energy into thinking up interesting applications, many of them involving devices he's made at home. (Willingham, 2009, p. 64-65)

Clearly, the instructors above have found a style that works for each one of them. It fits their personalities. Students respond warmly. Style matters to students. However, the contrarian would point out that whether or not a student finds a class enjoyable, pleasant, comforting, entertaining or otherwise attractive; it does not matter as much as whether they are engaged in deep learning. As Willingham points out, and I would agree: If there is an emotional bond between the students and the instructor, then it can help to facilitate an effective platform to stimulate deep learning.

I know of a fifth type of instructor. Teacher E is gruff, demanding, somewhat boring, and dreaded by the students. This is Professor Kingsley in the 1973 movie about law school, *The Paper Chase*. Yet, this professor somehow gets the students to respect her or him greatly. There is that effective emotional bond, similar to what Willingham points out.

The point is that style matters a great deal and fortunately many different styles will cultivate respect and thus work to nurture an emotional bond. Instructors need to find a style that works for their personality and perhaps the most important credo about personal style is to be oneself. There is nothing more inspiring than to demonstrate a style and approach that is real. Even if the instructor is quite different in age, culture, or personal background from the students; a style that is a genuine reflection of the individual can be most effective. If the style is easily understood by the students, the instructor can be more approachable. If the style is quite different from what students have known, then it can broaden their understanding and appreciation of cultural differences. Beyond being genuine, instructors need to realize that their style is important to prime the students for deep learning. Does the instructor exude passion for the material that the student can think about, and ask questions about? If students are only entertained or if they only like one's individual affect, personality, or clothing selections; that is not enough. Indeed, it may even be a distraction if students remember the style without it leading them to deep learning.

Hence, style matters as it can function to help build interest and connect students to caring about the material. The traditional academic style is to have things clean; e.g., presentations and written materials, like the scholarly journals mentioned above, center on black and white text. The traditional approach is to give content without embellishments or distractions so that the inherent interest of the material directs the attention of the scholar. In contrast, some contemporary instructors are trying to add a little bling and a few jokes in the hope that it will keep students entertained. I support this new concern for classroom style, yet adding a few jokes or a stab at entertainment does not go far enough unless it builds interest in the material leading to more deep learning.

What is it about some teaching styles that makes them effective in building student interest in the class? This leads to a more central question, what makes doing anything interesting? If we wish to assert that the character and style of the experience helps to make some activities more interesting, it begs yet another question, what do we mean by interesting? I find that there is significant ambiguity in the term interesting. There are three meanings of interesting in a classroom context: 1) The pleasant and inviting style of the class makes it interesting. The instructor is lovable. There are jokes and students are entertained. 2) The material is interesting because it connects to areas that the students already know about and like. Ergo it would follow that instructors should vie to teach classes on topics students may think to be attractive inherently; for example, film studies rather than my own area, the acoustics of speech. 3) When classes are full of engaging tasks inherent in reflective practice, they can be interesting. As with the examples of jigsaw puzzles and crossword puzzles, interest can be generated by critical thinking and the pleasures of problem solving it creates. Such problem solving develops and refines the tools to address even more problems and to do it more effectively. Intrinsic rewards are recognized. Deep learning becomes attractive.

The point is that being a showman can be good, but like the extrinsic rewards of giving a child a gold star in a music lesson, it is good only because it is a leads to larger intrinsic rewards of deep learning. Inspiring classes are interesting because the activities involve problem solving. With regard to the second point above, one cannot expect to design a viable curriculum around only what students might have found attractive prior to the course. This would limit students from getting interested in new topics. The content integral to the college curriculum is not necessarily designed or expected to align with the interests of entering students. Perhaps more importantly, the inherent interest in the content the student has prior to taking a course usually doesn't matter much, because the intrinsic rewards of deep learning can be powerful and overcome prior ideas about what is of interest. As stated in an earlier chapter, one can learn to love shit.

How do we structure courses for problem solving to increase the likelihood that its intrinsic interest will entice students to care about the material and seek out deep learning? Unfortunately, I have observed that many instructors do not think enough about leading students to deep learning when designing courses. Here are some considerations about content and style that I have observed from traditional instructors:

- Traditional instructors spend a great deal of time making sure that what they cover everything important in an area. The instructors want to make the impression that they are comprehensive and complete. There is a sense of obligation that students should have been exposed to material without regard to whether it is retained and used for far transfer. They don't realize that including too much material is a bad thing.

- If an instructor has difficulty explaining a challenging concept or is concerned that the students might find an area intimidating, she or he minimizes or omits material rather than restructuring it into meaningful challenges matching student abilities and scaffolding it to build understanding and thus intrinsic rewards.

- Sometimes instructors think that students will respect them more if they appear scholarly and academic. As a result, lectures are filled with allusions to primary sources and scholarly references in the expectation that the material will appear well vetted and researched. This seldom impresses undergraduate students.

- It can be common for instructors to worry about whether they are going to appear to the students as knowing the content and being in control of the material. Indirectly, the instructors can't help but show off about how much knowledge and insight they have about their topic. Students are typically poor judges of an instructor's scholarly understanding. Students assume the instructor knows more about the subject than they do. Beyond that, they typically don't know or care

much about an instructor's background, accomplishments, or
scholarly credentials.

- Many instructors are convinced that their topic will have an important
  impact on society that should compel students to care and to learn it.
  But asserting this, by itself, does not necessarily persuade students
  that this is the case, nor does it foster their deep learning.

- Because it is assumed that being entertaining is good, jokes are
  inserted into lectures. But instructors are mistaken if they confuse
  getting a few laughs with enticing students to like the material. The
  best entertainment is derived from the intrinsic rewards of pursuing
  and commanding an understanding of the material—and having ones
  interest piqued by new questions that are discovered in this quest.

The contrarian might suggest that these considerations concentrate too
much on the values of the instructor. Rather than being too concerned with the
considerations in the above list, instructors should be most concerned about
whether they are making a genuine, emotional, and personal connection with
the students that will lead students to ask and seek answers to questions on
their own.

In discussing generational differences between students and instructors,
Diana Oblinger (2003) asserted that we should design learning experiences
with a form and style that appeals to the student, not the instructor. As she
pointed out "An essential component of facilitating learning is understanding
learners" (p. 37). How many of the items on the list above were oriented to the
students' values in a way that would help with an emotional connection to the
instructor and how many were more focused on what the instructor thought
was important? My opinion is that instructors could do well by concentrating
less about content and more about connecting with students on the students'
level. Students can learn academic style later when, as deep learners, they
might then care more about it.

Here is an example. As we start a class, even on the first day, how can we
begin to connect with the students? First impressions do matter (Matejka &
Kupka, 1994), yet the first day of class is often devoted to an overview of the
course, and specifically a review of the syllabus is almost ubiquitous. Students
are not engaged in reflective practice yet. The students receive the information
about the mechanics of the class, and if they do have any questions, their
questions are about expectations, scoring, and grading. The questions reflect a
strategic-learning mode. In contrast, Ludy, Brackenbury, Folkins, Peet,
Langendorfer, & Beining (2016) have explained that producing a syllabus

designed to engage students can be a useful way to begin a positive connection between the students and the instructor. Begin the first class period and the syllabus with stimulating questions raised from the material to be covered, not the mechanics of the class. Further, an instructor might ask: What do students like? How do I connect with them? If students are more comfortable with the format of a web page or a magazine article than they are with a structured academic piece, instructors should design a syllabus to account for that.

As reviewed by Ludy et al. (2016) there are a number of types of syllabus. The traditional syllabus is the most academic in nature. It is black and white, concise, and provides information in an organized and helpful way. Over the last few decades, there has been pressure to make the syllabus more of a tool to ensure that students are fully informed about course requirements, expectations, disability access, and prohibitions such as cheating or academic dishonesty[67]. As a result, a second general type of syllabus has evolved, the contractual syllabus. The contractual syllabus is like the traditional syllabus, yet much more comprehensive, and in places it is effusive. The emphasis is not on providing information to the students as much as it is with having a written record documenting that students have been informed. A third type of syllabus is the learner-centered syllabus that has garnered interest in the last few years (Grunert Obrien, Millis, & Cohen, 2008). The learner-centered syllabus tries to connect with the students, to interest them in the class as participants in the learning to be done, and to empower them with the knowledge that they have choices about their own learning. As one might expect, I love the learner-centered syllabus. However, Ludy et al. have gone a step further. Following Nilson's (1998) assertion that a syllabus might "not only be a road map for the term's foray into knowledge, but also a travelogue to pique students' interest in the expedition" (p. 19). We developed a number of variations in the syllabus to follow Diana Oblinger's (2003) prodding to connect with the student. We call this the engaging syllabus, and as a variation on the learner-centered syllabus it features elements of appealing graphic design, a focus on students and the questions they may ask, and an explanation of the course as a deep learning experience. Content is included, but it is embedded in an appealing package. An engaging syllabus will have style. It will be visually appealing with lots of color, fonts and banners set with visual design expertise (Williams, 2008), tables, side bars, charts, pictures, and links

---

[67] I admit, when I was a Provost I worked hard to ensure that faculty members had comprehensive lists of itemized requirements in their syllabus. The General Counsel for the university insisted on it.

to web pages[68]. Most importantly, the engaging syllabus is designed to stimulate students to begin developing their own questions about the material of the course.

In the spirit of Boyer (1990), Ludy et al. (2016) decided to study the syllabus as a scholarly topic. What aspects of a syllabus will make a difference? An ideal study would be to test to see if students really do engage in more deep learning after taking a class with an engaging syllabus versus another type of syllabus. As with many areas of our lives, it didn't seem practical to do such a study. However, Ludy et al. were able to take the same content describing a class and put it into both a contractual syllabus and an engaging syllabus. Examples of these syllabus types are shown in color in the Ludy et al. paper at http://digitalcommons.georgiasouthern.edu/cgi/viewcontent.cgi?article=1634&context=ij-sotl.

We gave the contractual syllabus to one section of an introductory nutrition class and the engaged syllabus to a matching class section, with a combined enrollment of 368 students. Each class section completed a survey to assess what they thought of each syllabus. 91% of the students liked the contractual syllabus and 96% liked the engaging syllabus. This was not surprising as Ludy et al. went to some effort to construct both syllabi well. The students in the engaging syllabus class section thought their syllabus was much more visually appealing than the students in the other class section. This is also not surprising. Ludy et al. designed the engaging syllabus to be like that. What we found most interesting, and what I think is important relative to developing the bond between student and instructor, is that in comparison to the class section with the contractual syllabus, the engaging syllabus section judged the instructor as more approachable/personable, creative/interesting, encouraging/caring for students, enthusiastic, flexible/open-minded, happy/positive, knowledgeable, prepared, current, and realistic/fair. It is remarkable that on the first day the students' impressions of the syllabus influenced their view of the instructor so directly. Perhaps even more importantly, the students reported that they thought the engaging syllabus motivated them to wish to learn more about the content.

---

[68] One might note that in the future syllabi are expected to be fully integrated into the web and course management systems. For now, one still needs to have a paper syllabus; but links, QR codes, and photos that come to life on a smart phone when scanned are options.

Chapter 12

SPACE MATTERS

THE CONTRARIAN INSTRUCTOR AND THE CLASSROOM

The contrarian instructor would remind us that the characteristics determining the success of any course are not necessarily related to how the material is selected or presented. The most essential characteristics relate to how the instructor designs a course to provide a student experience built on reflective practice that cultivates deep learning. This student experience is influenced by many factors, such as the style of the instructor or the style of the syllabus discussed in the previous chapter. Another one of the factors influencing the student experience is the learning environment; and in this case I specifically mean the design and character of the classroom. Traditional instructors may often give little to no thought about the characteristics and functionality of the classroom assigned—or if they do, the instructors assume it is beyond their control.

In contrast, the contrarian instructor will have a great deal of concern for the environment well ahead of the beginning of the semester and will take an active role in advocating for such factors as: Can students and instructors hear and see each other from all around the classroom? Are there distractions? Is it a pleasant environment, maybe even with some style and charm? What facilitates communication and with whom? How does the space influence what is done inside of class and how does it stimulate the best learning experience? How does the space promote moving students from strategic to deep learning? This chapter is a summary of a more in depth study of the instructor's role in advocating for classroom design to facilitate learning by Folkins, Friberg, & Cesarini (2015) and the reader is referred to that paper for a more detailed discussion of each topic.

Architects have defined formal classroom types: 1) seminar room with table in the middle, 2) small-to-medium size classroom with loose seating, 3) larger classroom with fixed seating including lecture halls with 50 to 150 seats, 4) collaborative classrooms with tables for active learning, and 5) large auditoriums. These classrooms are designed to fit the variety of different class structures; however, it is not always possible to match the design of the classroom to the design of the class. Further, different instructors may take quite different approaches to teaching the same course. Yet, usually classroom assignments are based solely on matching enrollment and seating capacity. We need to do more. The functioning of the classroom must fit the needs of the students given how the course has been organized by the instructor. If the classroom doesn't fit how the instructor plans to use the space, it is up to the instructor to find a different classroom, modify an existing classroom, or to redesign the course in a manner that facilitates learning in the space available. The fundamental point is that the instructor cannot be neutral in terms of the functioning of the classroom space. As explained in the initial chapters of this book, instructors have a responsibility, not just to teaching, but to student learning. The space matters. In the words of architect Patrick Poulter (1994):

> Space is neither innocent nor neutral. It is an instrument of the political; it has a performative aspect for whoever inhabits it; it works on its occupants. At the micro level, space prohibits, decides what may occur, lays down the law, implies a certain order, commands and locates bodies (p. 175).

Unfortunately, if a classroom space does not function well many instructors seem to assume that nothing can be done. If they do complain, the complaints tend to be directed to fellow instructors. Instructors seldom make the effort to ask the administration to change classroom characteristics to fit their needs, especially if they are embarking on new teaching approaches. Instructors should speak up as university administrators, space planners, and architects care greatly about providing facilities that are effective for learning. They are keenly interested in knowing about what makes a better classroom. However, even though these other groups care, they might not be able to accommodate requests as designing and rehabilitating classrooms is always a compromise among many different factors. Usually, instructors are only aware of their own needs, but the funding for renovation must be found from among many financial demands and when it is, there are always compromises with fire codes, long and short term maintenance costs, maximizing space utilization, and more. Like too many administrative decisions, the choices made to provide good classrooms are the result of a complex web of rules, regulations, plans for the future, and relations among those in the positions to advocate for and make decisions. Instructors must work hard to be influential in this regard. They can remind decision-makers that classrooms must function first and foremost for student learning. That is, after all, why the classrooms are there. The contrarian would assert that classrooms should be functional learning spaces envisioned primarily by instructors and developed collaboratively by instructors, administrators, and architects.

LECTURE HALLS

As stated many times in earlier chapters, lectures have long been a staple of the university experience. Some prognosticators have suggested that technology and active learning techniques will soon supplant the lecture. I have heard this off-and-on for about 20 years. Earlier I mentioned that in the 1990s, one of the Regents for the state universities in Iowa advocated for a moratorium on building classrooms and lecture halls of all sorts, as online learning technology was soon to make them outdated. Although lectures are sure to evolve with the times and opportunities, I expect they will persist to some extent as they have done for millennia. One or more persons speaking to a large group of listeners is just too engrained in what we expect as a society. Lecturing can work well for many learning experiences, but typically it is most effective when students are already in a deep-learning mode.

Interestingly, today's lecture halls can benefit from features somewhat different from the traditional auditorium. For example, even if seating is fixed, students need desk space wide enough for technology as well as a writing surface. It is still possible to have student discussion groups in a fixed seating auditorium; some accommodate this better than others. For example, if there are a number of empty seats, students can be assigned to teams that are required to sit together. By sitting in a "U" shape with one or two open seats in the middle, five or seven students can form a discussion team even with fixed auditorium seats (Folkins, 2010). This works better if there are also empty seats between groups of students. Yet, instructors can meet significant resistance from practical constraints on the administration if they insist that an auditorium they are using be limited to two-thirds capacity.

AISLES AND HALLWAYS

The location of aisles is another example of how an auditorium's design can influence instruction. A lot of instructors like to move around during class whether engaged in a lecture activity or not, but many auditoria are designed in a way that the instructor is confined to a stage area. This is a significant concern if students are divided into discussion groups and instructors, teaching assistants, and peer facilitators wish to visit different groups. For years, I preferred to teach in an older auditorium rather than a newer one as the older room had a wide center aisle for the peer facilitators and me to move about easily.

One of the few relatively ubiquitous characteristics of universities across the nation is that there is approximately 10 minutes between classes and classes are scheduled back-to-back throughout the day for efficiency. Unfortunately, this is often not enough time for students to pick up their belongings and navigate out along a crowded aisle often while talking with friends. The students need to exit before students for the next class can come in. Yet, the aisles are so narrow that there is always a traffic jam. Instructors should be available for student questions and discussions before and after class. Instructors also need to log-off of their technology and collect their materials. I had a friend and colleague at another university who would stand at the door and shake hands and socialize with each student as he or she left a graduate class, just like a minister would do after a church service. This instructor found this greeting at the door an effective way to enhance connection with his students. Unfortunately, though, the instructor for the next class also needed to get in, set up, and have the opportunity to meet with students ahead of time. The contrarian instructor would assert that these interstitial times are exactly what is needed to foster deep learning. Yet, the narrow aisles and doors make the paltry ten minutes not nearly enough time to take full advantage of what can be done to connect with students.

There is an alternative. The contrarian instructor realizes that the space outside of the classroom doors can be more than a hallway to move people in and out. It can be a place to congregate. I liked to come to class early, stand outside the door as the previous class was finishing, and socialize with the students. Many times I would purposely linger in the hallway afterward. Many students are more comfortable asking questions in this informal setting than doing so in class. Coming to class early and leaving late are more comfortable for students than going to office hours[69]. If one does it right, the students will soon recognize that this is when the professor is easily accessible. Word spreads to come early and stay late. The environment facilitates students moving into a deep learning mode. Do students have their own questions? Can they get direction from the instructor about how to seek out answers to these questions and to get stimulation to ask more questions?

Can we, as contrarian instructors, make sure that the hallway spaces outside of classrooms are conductive to such learning? Many classrooms open up to sterile hallways full of traffic and without chairs or benches. Yet, more and more buildings are being designed or remodeled for student gathering spaces outside of classrooms. Such spaces include comfortable chairs, furniture groupings to facilitate discussions, white boards or walls that can be used as white boards, and even handy technology. The contrarian instructor can make good use of these spaces to foster deep learning and that will go a long way to justify the architectural changes needed to make them inviting.

ACTIVE LEARNING CLASSROOMS

One of the most significant characteristics of contrarian learning has been the shift to active-learning classrooms. The traditional approach suggests that classes with large enrollments are for lecturing and that classes with small enrollments can be centered around discussion. The contrarian would assert that active participation in discussion should be central to both classes with small and large enrollments. With a small class, students can interact with an instructor and it is easy to switch between lecture and discussion modes. In a large class, it is impractical for students to ask questions during a lecture other than to ask the instructor for clarification, repetition, or to slow down. Consequently, for larger classes one must be deliberate in setting up group activities so that students can be engaged through discussions.

---

[69] When I was a Provost I was expected to send out regular reminders to faculty members that it was required to hold office hours. As a contrarian, I can now admit that the idea of office hours doesn't work very often. Traditional faculty members make sure they are available for office hours; they are told to do so. Yet students seldom come. Many students believe there is a stigma connected to going to office hours. It is admitting they are having difficulty. Although I think faculty members should take the responsibility for attracting students to their office hours, holding office hours is not effective enough to justify the time and expense. Connecting with students before and after class may be more practical.

A number of studies show that effective classroom design can contribute significantly to students' ability to engage in active learning (Hill & Epps, 2010; Walker, Brooks, & Baepler, 2011; Brooks, 2012, and Sawyer, 2014). As the classroom is flipped so that new material is presented outside of class and reflective practice occurs during class time, it is more important to design the space for discussion and debate among students, and to allow instructors to move in and out of such discussions. A classroom designed to accommodate groups of students is best, but auditoria that are unfriendly to grouping students can be adapted.

Many classrooms are now being constructed to facilitate active learning. They have students seated at tables. Some have more technology than others. Many factors can go into the design of the technology: Are the groups using technology to report out to the class? Does one need high-speed video at each table? Is there a mix between lectures using technology and the students' use of technology at the table? Is it necessary to fix the placement of the tables with cables to allow some of the more demanding technologies? To me, the technology does not drive the design as the technology will be changing continuously. Today more and more classes are having students use their own notebook computers, tablets, or smartphones; cutely named bring-your-own-device or BYOD, which simplifies design of classroom-based technology considerably.

What is important is flexibility. Different instructors will wish to use the technology differently and the technology will change and evolve much faster than the classroom infrastructure will be able to change. One should also recognize that sometimes there are advantages to a low-technology approach. For example, small portable white boards called huddle boards can be held up for each group to present their work to the class. Instead of having students choose one of four options for response during a lecture by making an entry with their smartphone, students hold up colored cards. The colored cards have the advantage that the students can look around the room and see how their peers responded. Of course, sometimes confidentiality is desirable and other times it is not, which is the point of being flexible.

Some instructors prefer small groups of two or three students, others like large groups. Michaelson, Bauman Knight, & Fink (2003) have shown that groups of about five to seven students are optimal. However, one needs to allow variation. Small tables can be moved into pods of two, three, or four to allow a variety of configurations thus accommodating innovation in how groups are aligned and employed for different activities. Tables on wheels can be rearranged easily between classes.[70]

Generally, floors should be flat if tables are to be used, but it is possible to create rooms with tiers wide enough for one or two tables. If chairs are on wheels, the tiered grouping of tables can be realigned easily for classes to switch instantly from lecture to group activity. The dinner shows in Las Vegas are in rooms with tables on tiers. They are an example of a room design that is a compromise between auditorium configuration and table seating. Many banquet halls or multipurpose rooms have an elevated stage with tables below on a flat floor. This allows the unobstructed view of the stage one gets from the back of an elevated auditorium, but with a flat floor. This design can work well for active learning classrooms as students in the back can still see, but the flat floor facilitates rearranging tables and chairs and moving between tables.

Regardless of the alignment of tables, it should be pointed out that one of the most important characteristics of any design is that students should be able to communicate with each other easily. Many classes are taught in rooms using the traditional banquet-hall table that is six feet in diameter. Banquet hall designers and managers prefer this size as it accommodates four couples at each table. However, this table-size puts the heads, more importantly the ears, of students on opposite sides about eight feet apart. At this distance, students cannot hear due to the background noise from other tables. At banquets, this table size often splits the conversation between two different sides of the table. I find this annoying at banquets. I find this to be an even more significant problem for discussion classrooms. If one is limited to six-foot tables, try to place them as far apart as possible.

Traditionally, medium and smaller classrooms have movable chairs with tablet arms. These chairs quickly get out of alignment, but the most significant problem is that space planners put too many chairs in each classroom so that one cannot rearrange the class easily and one cannot set up groups of tablet-arm chairs with space to move between them. Another limitation of tablet-arm chairs is that the tablets are too small to both write and use technology. There are newer tablet-arm chairs available that have a larger work surface, can switch easily between right and left handed use, and have storage for bags underneath. In practice, I have found that the tablets are still too small and that students will leave backpacks and other items between chairs even with

---

[70] The article by Folkins, Friberg, and Cesarini (2015) provides much more specificity for the interested reader. For example, should tables be round, rectangular, trapezoidal, or some other configuration? There are advantages to each option.

storage underneath. One of the advantages of some tablet-arm chair designs is that extras can be folded and stacked in the corner to make the space more flexible when classrooms are not at capacity.

The contrarian would point out that in general, students can work better in class when seated at tables rather than tablet-arm chairs. There is more space for students to spread out materials, they have a common writing area, and the tables generally make discussions easier to maintain. It is best when there are wheels on both the chairs and tables so that configurations can be changed and unused tables can be moved away allowing more space between the tables in use. It is important to have large spaces between tables so that conversations will not interfere across tables, and to allow instructors and students to move easily between tables.

CLASSROOM SHAPE

In general, the traditional classroom is rectangular. The older classrooms all had the head of the class at one of the ends; that is, along one of the shorter walls. The problem is that the students in the back are at a significant disadvantage. Even if they can see and hear, they do not have the experience of being as close to the teacher as those in the front. Classrooms with a high aspect ratio, that is they are narrow and deep, exacerbate this.

Newstock (2014) contrasts the concept of distance learning with a term he favors, close learning, which emphasizes the "laborious, time-consuming, and costly but irreplaceable proximity between teacher and student" (page 5). Following the logic that sitting at the end of a log with Socrates at the other end is the best close learning, a student sitting in the second row of a class does not have the optimal close learning experience.[71] Although this perspective takes the issue too far, one can feel at a disadvantage when stuck in the back row, especially in a long and narrow classroom. In response, it is now common to find classrooms with the front aligned along one of the longer walls. The disadvantage here is that students along the sides do not have good sight lines. Again, extreme aspect ratios; that is classrooms that are wide and shallow, make this worse. Students at the side can have a poor angle to view

---

[71] It is interesting to think that Newstock's (2014) concern for close learning makes the second row distance learning, and improvements in technology now allow distance learning to expand the back row of the classroom out for thousands of miles.

the two-dimensional image on a screen at the front. The compromise of putting extra screens along the sides of the front wall is less than ideal in that students sitting on the side often need to switch sight lines between the screen and the instructor.

Through the years, I have taught in classrooms of all shapes. I much prefer a square classroom, with an aspect ratio of 1:1. This is the best compromise between minimizing those in the back and having good sightlines. Unfortunately, classrooms are often designed with an aspect ratio that fits the available space in a building. Instead, one should begin by designing classrooms with a desired size and aspect ratio and then creating the design for the rest of the building around that. The contrarian instructor is more interested in how a classroom performs than what a building looks like[72].

Large auditoriums and lecture halls have a stage at the front providing a clear focus and sight lines from all seats. Large rooms with tables for active learning are sometimes de-centered with no clear focus. In this case there may be screens distributed around the room for a closer view. However, many times an instructor may wish to use a combination of active-learning activities and demonstrations to the class as a whole. In this case, the lack of a clear focus in the front can be awkward as students need to look one direction to see a screen and another to see the presenter.

Some instructors like to speak from behind a large podium with space for notes and an array of monitors and controls for technology close at hand. Others prefer a smaller podium or even to avoid a podium as podiums symbolically block the instructor from the class. Without the podium, instructors can move around the room to improve close learning and they can still control the technology with a hand-held remote. As long as wireless technology is available, podiums on wheels can be moved to a corner. Movable podiums can also be used to rearrange the head of the room and the student sightlines as table configurations are changed. The contrarian's point is that the design of the head of the classroom and the podiums are examples of the larger issue--classrooms must be designed with flexibility to accommodate the style and approach the instructor wishes to use.

---

[72] Modernist architects have followed Louis Sullivan's credo: form follows function. This is interpreted to mean that the form of a building should follow it functional purpose. If the classrooms are a primary function of a building, then the overall design of a building should not require compromises like classrooms with extreme aspect ratios or other less functional shapes due to the need to fit the classrooms into the space available.

SOUND AND LIGHT

Much of my scholarly background is in the acoustics of speech and hearing, and so it is appropriate that a major point in this chapter is about communication. Classrooms are designed for people to speak and to hear. What the classrooms look like is important. The style and character of classrooms is important. Moving around before and after class, as well as connecting as close learners is important. But none of these factors are as important as everyone being able to communicate with everyone else from anywhere in the room. When one person says something, all others need to both hear and understand it. When students ask questions or student groups report their work to the class, every other student and the instructor need to be able to hear and understand. If a student is straining to hear or understand what is said, then she or he is distracted from the work of deep learning. Further, as the American Speech-Language-Hearing Association has provided guidance, an optimal listening environment is especially important for "young students, English language-learners, and students and teachers with hearing, language, or learning problems" (American Speech-Language-Hearing Association, 2005, p. 1). That is, students with the greatest communication challenges are most impacted by poor room acoustics. Being required to speak loudly in class may also lead to vocal abuse for instructors (Titze, 2010).

The American Speech-Language-Hearing Association (2005) has issued minimum standards for classroom listening environments: 1) the background noise should not exceed 35 dB, 2) the intensity of any speech produced in comparison to the background noise, called the signal-to-noise ratio, should be at least +15 dB, and 3) the reverberation in the room should be less than 0.6 seconds for small classrooms and less than 0.7 seconds for larger classrooms. Further, classrooms are not uniform listening environments, as a result some locations in the room may meet these standards and other places might not. Unfortunately, few classrooms meet the American Speech-Hearing-Language Association standards in any part of the room (Crandall & Smalldino, 1995; Knecht et al., 2002). For example, most ventilation systems produce noise levels well over 35 dB[73]. Reverberation may cause some of the most significant issues; for example, when rooms are narrow with low ceilings and

---

[73] There are a number of free smart phone and tablet apps available that allow one to make a crude measure of the background noise level and the signal to noise ratio.

the walls, floor, and ceiling have glossy surfaces, the reverberation makes it easy to detect a sound, but quite difficult to understand what is being said.

What can be done when classroom acoustics are poor? The traditional instructors will typically complain to students or colleagues, then they will try to talk louder. The contrarian instructor will be a public and tireless advocate for four themes: 1) instructors must learn to pay attention and care more about how every classroom performs for communication, 2) acoustic performance should be important design criteria for classrooms, 3) instructors should use a microphone when speaking to even the smallest class, and 4) students who have questions need quick access to wireless microphones anywhere in class. President Lincoln gave the Gettysburg Address to over 9000 people in an outside venue in an era before microphones were available. Few of us have Lincoln's rhetorical prowess. Use a microphone.

Although from my perspective acoustics are most important for communication, classroom lighting is also a concern. Students must be able to see the instructor, the visual displays, their work in front of them, and other students. Lighting also sets the tone and influences the atmosphere in a room. Architects have long recognized the difficulties of controlling the lighting in classroom spaces. Electronic displays can be washed out if the room is too bright and glare can often be a problem from the placement of lights. If the lighting is too low, the students snooze.

It is common for new classrooms to come with complex zoned lighting. It is not unusual to find lighting control boards where an instructor can scroll down a dozen different lighting combinations. The problem is that instructors often wish to control the lighting on the fly; that is, instructors want to change the lighting at the front or the back of a room in the middle of a sentence without causing a disruption. Scrolling through preprogrammed lighting options is adequate for choosing a combination at the beginning of class. It works poorly for changing the lighting in the middle of class when it disrupts other activities. Rather than preset lighting combinations, I prefer to have a separate switch for each zone. Then I can easily change lighting without thinking too much.

These separate switches should be easy to find in the dark or low light. It is best to have switches all around the room and some switches should be by the doors allowing a dark room to be lit without searching for the podium. Some switches should be in the front of the room or at the podium for quick access during a lecture. A good solution is to have lighting control on a portable remote so the instructor can easily carry it around. No excuse justifies interrupting learning while the instructor struggles to adjust classroom lighting, yet that is commonly what happens with one central control for zoned lighting.

Windows have long functioned to provide ventilation and light in rooms of all sorts. With the advent of air conditioning, a trend developed to build rooms such as laboratories, auditoria, and clinical facilities of many types without windows. Windows were seen as unnecessary and undesirable as they were a source of light that had to be controlled, a potential distraction for people working or conducting meetings, a drain on heat and cooling resources, and, perhaps most tellingly, an extra expense to build and maintain. This trend for windowless rooms soon spread to become common for classrooms.

Yet, windows make a significant difference in how people perceive a room. We all know that windows are essential in building a home, and usually we want more and more windows in our homes. Office space with windows is prized, especially the corner office. Conference rooms with windows can set a good tone for a meeting. It seems that the concern for distractions from windows is over rated; or at least when people are distracted and begin to gaze out the window it can tell us that what is going on in the room is not keeping their interest. Hence the contrarian would insist that we need to put windows in our classrooms. They provide a positive and inviting atmosphere. They add interest to the classroom space. Glare or unwanted light can be controlled; i.e., one could have a single hand-held remote to control the lighting, window shades, and audio settings. Even classroom windows that open to a hallway or other indoor space can improve the tone and feel of a classroom. Of course, one also needs a small window in the door or next to the door so that those in the hallway can see if a class is in session prior to opening the door.

CLASSROOM DESIGN PRINCIPLES

The classroom design principles presented in this chapter are explained in more detail by Folkins, Friberg, & Cesarini (2015). The main point is that contrarian instructors need to learn about what makes an effective classroom space and understand that it is their responsibility to advocate effectively for spaces that work for their students to learn. Architects have any number of other factors to consider when designing classrooms, such as locating the rooms properly in a building or the costs of both building and maintaining the classrooms. Architects do a great job, but they do not have the first-hand information about student learning that instructors have. The point is not to give advice to architects, but to inspire contrarian instructors to take the initiative to lobby in support of their own interests in student learning.

The Folkins, Friberg, & Cesarini (2015) paper concludes with a number of design principles that may be useful for instructors to consider. These principles are quoted below to inspire other contrarian instructors to develop their own lists:

1. Seating must be flexible to accommodate different activities and arrangements, especially to allow students to interact in groups of different sizes. Although large classrooms tend to have fixed auditorium-style seating, flexible seating is more important as the classroom gets larger or the number of students enrolled in a course increases.

2. There should be space for the instructor to move around from group-to-group or student-to-student, regardless of how classroom seating is arranged. If fixed seating is necessary, have lot of aisles to allow free movement, especially down the middle of the room.

3. Students in groups should have a way to report out to the rest of the class, either through classroom technology, bring-your-own-device (BYOD), or huddle boards. Technology should be wireless so that seating options are not limited by hard-wired connectivity issues.

4. There should be a clear focal point to the room, with good sight lines from all seating arrangements. Podiums should be easily movable to allow flexibility. Students should not be looking in different directions to view a projected display and a presenter.

5. Acoustics are central to communication, especially for those with communication challenges. Attention should be given to signal-to-noise levels as well as reverberation to maximize classroom communication. Instructors should be able to talk to the entire class from any location. Students at any location should be able to ask questions or report out from a group and be heard by everyone.

6. Simple zoned lighting works well and should be adjustable easily from different points in the room.

7. Classrooms should be easily accessible as time between classes is often at a premium. This can be facilitated with wide aisles and wide doors.

8. Spaces should be available for students to congregate outside the classroom before and after class. These spaces should also have good acoustics to facilitate discussion.

9.   Windows are not the enemy. Windows can add interest, character, and
     style to classroom spaces. Interior windows can often add to the
     classroom appeal as well as minimizing interruptions when windows
     are next to or in the door.

Chapter 13

LEARNING LEADERSHIP IN EVERY COURSE

LEARNING HOW TO LEAD

Imagine you are in a store. A band of disaffected professors comes in and loudly announces: "This is a hold up!" A clerk quickly hits a concealed alarm button. The police are on their way and it becomes clear that the robbery is foiled. The disaffected professors don't wish to be caught and they decide to take the customers in the store as hostages. The customers are moved into a back room and the door is locked[74]. The hostages must now decide what to do and, if they can develop a plan to negotiate with the robbers, they need to decide who among them might direct the negotiations. The hostages are all strangers to each other. Who will become their leader? It is unlikely that the hostages will take a vote in this situation unless there is some conflict among them. Rather, it is most likely than one or two individuals will emerge with both the best ideas about what to do and behaviors that will be favored by the group for any negotiation.

The hostages who are most influential in the scenario above are what DePree (1989) calls roving leaders. Roving leaders do not have titles or formal positions of authority. Instead, roving leaders are the types of individuals who will rise to leadership challenges on the basis of their ability to be respected, influential, and convincing in their arguments; i.e., the quality of their critical thinking as well as how they use the reflective practice skills of communication, collaboration, and cooperation to interact with others in the

---

[74]One would hope that the back room is not a walk-in freezer or a bank safe.

group. In my opinion, these traits of the roving leader are often easy to recognize. Indeed, the contrarian would point out that instead of getting a formal leadership position and then using the position to give directions to others, many leaders are recognized for their roving leadership abilities and only later are they promoted to formal positions of leadership. I have known many college deans, provosts, and presidents throughout my career and almost all of them would be the type of person to take charge naturally when in a group of hostages. Many other people will not get formal leadership positions; but they are often in situations where they take on a roving leadership role. Such leadership is a valuable skill. It is not just to lead a group of hostages; it is fundamental to a great number of human interactions. For those of us who wish to make a difference with our lives, to contribute to society or improve life on Earth[75], leadership skill is essential. The point of this chapter is that leadership is tightly connected to the values and attributes of a liberal education. Although it is not on the list of purposes for college provided by Thomas Jefferson in Chapter Two, learning to be a roving leader is an important reason for gaining a liberal education.

Leadership belongs throughout the undergraduate curriculum. Why are we developing thoughtful, inspired critical thinkers? It is for them to make a difference--a difference in their lives and most importantly in the lives of others. Some students arrive at college with a proclivity to lead. Others do not. It is easy to think of leadership as a fixed-entity trait. It is not. We all learn leadership incrementally. It is not enough to have critical thinking embedded throughout our students' learning activities. Students also need to learn to get beyond themselves and use their learning abilities to reach out. They can and will make a difference.

One of the joys of teaching graduate students is that many of them already recognize that they are working to prepare themselves for future leadership positions. It is easier to get graduate students than undergraduate students to understand the importance of developing and refining their leadership attributes. For a few years, I taught a course for doctoral students entitled, Pedagogy (Folkins, 2011). It was created originally to give these future faculty members a strong background in the practice and theory of college teaching. I loved teaching this course and in getting the students to reflect on and assess both traditional and contrarian approaches to teaching. But, I didn't stop there.

---

[75] As we know, improving life on Earth is a fundamentally human attribute not shared by other animals. Is it the most distinctive factor that separates us from other species?

The course had major components on the values, life-style, and expectations of a professor. As professing is to be their future vocation, it has always surprised me that so much of the doctoral curriculum is devoted to research and scholarship with so little attention to the many other aspects of faculty life[76]. Even further though, my course on college pedagogy included major components about leadership. Many of our doctoral students will go on to leadership positions not just in the classroom, but throughout academia. More importantly, faculty members are expected to play a leadership role in society. Once again I am putting learning goals above the importance of the content material in a course or discipline, but I think we need to prepare our graduate students for leadership that may cross disciplines.

What exactly is leadership? How does one define it? There is a large literature describing leadership skills. Many retired administrators, executives, military officers, politicians, and leaders of all sorts like to write books about leadership. A retired general, Sun Tzu, wrote *The Art of War*, one of the first leadership books, more than 2500 years ago. Niccolò Machiavelli, an ousted public administrator, wrote *The Prince*, one of the most influential books on leadership, 500 years ago. Both Sun Tzu and Machiavelli were clearly inspirational as contrarians. Yet it turns out that what is meant by leadership depends on who you read and what their theories about leadership are. Do they support transformational leadership (Burns, 1978), servant leadership (Greenleaf, 1970), relational leadership (Komives, Lucas, and McMahon, 2007), or one of the many other perspectives on leadership? Following DePree (1989) perhaps leadership is the ability to influence other people on the basis of, not a title or position of authority, but an individual's skill at critical thinking and persuasion. In many situations, leadership may involve overcoming confirmation bias. Yet, there is far too much significant ambiguity in such a description of leadership. Perhaps a better approach is to assert, as Supreme Court Justice Potter Stewart is purported to have said about obscenity, I can't define it explicitly, but "I know it when I see it[77]." Many of us can do a better job of spotting leadership than we can do of defining it.

There is good reason to expect that leadership styles differ across circumstances and personalities. What worked for Martin Luther might not have been an approach used by Martin Luther King, Jr. What about comparing the many leaders across all societies through history? Is there much that is

---

[76] Yet, in many regards doctoral students are learning this as reflective practitioners in their work as teaching and research assistants.

[77] It should be noted that Justice Steward had a significant visual impairment.

universal or are there a number of different approaches that have been effective? The personality aspects of leadership are referred to by Northouse (2013) as the trait approach and he has dubbed the variation across circumstances as the situational approach. Northouse explains that there is little consensus among the many concepts and approaches to studying leadership. Thus the leadership ideology and style useful for one individual to use in certain circumstances might be quite different than for another individual to use in other circumstances. Yet, there is a central point that has been shown over and over again—leadership can be learned (Northouse, 2013). It is a common misnomer that individuals can be naturally born as leaders. Incremental learning about leadership works. In spite of the admonitions of many shy or reticent people that they are not leaders: leadership is not a fixed entity or natural ability. The incremental approach to leadership development is one more reason that the contrarian would stress beginning with reflective practice. Reflective practice can accommodate individual differences and individual experimentation in learning leadership.

A related point is that students are not likely to learn to be leaders by listening to lectures about different theories of leadership. The discussion of reflective practice in Chapter Four stresses that one cannot learn a skill by just listening. It follows that one cannot learn to be wise by listing alone and one cannot learn to be a leader from only listening. Leadership grows from reflective practice that develops skills at critical thinking and using those skills: 1) to persuade and influence people, 2) to judge situations, 3) to notice and seize opportunities, and 4) to aspire to visions of a better world. Just as with mentoring students in their learning effective critical-thinking skills, instructors need to be deliberate in their efforts to encourage and guide students to develop leadership skills. Leadership can and should be included throughout the curriculum.

I have studied and taught leadership for a number of years. In my opinion, the general principles of leadership tend to arch across different disciplines and professional areas; e.g., there is reason to think that leading a business, a church, an army, a university, a class, an orchestra, and a garden club have many attributes in common (Zander & Zander, 2002). What are these general principles? Again, it depends on an individual's perspectives about what is important, who has influenced them, and their ideas about what leaders are supposed to accomplish. Because of this, there are many published lists of important skills and abilities one should cultivate to be an effective leader; see for example, Northouse (2013) or Kouzes & Posner (2012). Here is a list of approaches and actions that can promote leadership that I have developed and refined in teaching leadership through the years:

- Put values first. Learn people's views, values, strengths, and sensitivities. Express your own values in an open, general way. Live your values and make sure that your value-based actions are visible. Build trust in everyone knowing that both common and different values are understood and appreciated.
- Build a common vision. Begin with communication and common understandings of values. From there imagine and test new ideas about a grand new future (Big Hairy Audacious Goals or BHAGs, Collins & Porras, 1996). Build trust as all constituencies buy into the common vision.
- Practice low control, high responsibility. Lead, don't manage. When possible, give general guidance rather than explicit directions. Delegate early and often, but ensure that people's responsibilities match their skills and motivations. Give credit, but be open about accountability. Take the heat, not the credit.
- Make the hard decisions. The critical decisions belong to the leader, but should be made with as much information and advice as possible. Joint decision-making is important for many noncritical decisions. Sometimes timing is vital. Sometimes it is not.
- Leadership is a contact sport and so communication should be ubiquitous. Communicate early and often. Communicate about things that are important or may become important. Listen to responses and change visibly in response to input from others. Use a continuum of communication mediums from face-to-face to impersonal mass communication. Engage symbolism at every opportunity. Be inspiring. Build trust in everybody knowing that they are informed about what matters.
- Don't let positions get hardened. Everyone should be thinking change can happen anytime and anywhere. Don't openly disagree in a way that leads to confirmation bias and entrenchment. Don't let positions build to an argument. Use critical thinking, but do it in the right time and place. Build trust by tactfully letting people know where you stand.
- Create a leadership team. Always discuss significant decisions with confidants. Use mentors. Consult people new to the environment.

Consult people with ideas and backgrounds unlike your own. The team should expect to be consulted. Consult them. Support them. Follow up with debriefing and explore ideas to be more successful next time. Find ways to say thank you.

• Do not try to lead by invoking authority, promising extrinsic rewards, threatening punishment, begging, or forcefully trying to impose a conclusion that seems logical to you. Instead, lead with the processes given above.

Are these the best principles? What are the reasons, evidence, assumptions, and significant ambiguities one can analyze in deciding to adopt them? Scholars, as well as leaders and commentators of all sorts, have debated leadership principles over the centuries. Volumes have been written on the topic. Reviewing that evidence is not practical in this book and it would not really address the points being made. I have found that these principles work for me. It is up to the reader to do her or his own analysis and evaluation. This is also the lesson for putting leadership in the curriculum. Having students practice leadership, and reflect on their actions and improve them, is much more powerful than giving a lecture surveying leadership theories.

The astute reader might also have observed that, although the points above come from experience with leadership, they are very similar to the points made about learning in the earlier sections of this book. Leadership is essentially the practice of using ones own deep learning to influence the deep learning of others. These principles reflect the approach I have tried to take in writing this book.

LEARNING WHERE TO LEAD — A TWIST

At the beginning of this book there is a list of contrarian teaching principles. One of them was, when it is practical, instructors can put something unanticipated, a twist, at the end of what the student was expecting to learn[78]. It is difficult and perhaps distracting to make a twist that is a dramatic surprise, but a new idea that was not foreshadowed can add interest. This book has

---

[78] Many traditional instructors will reject this approach. They tell students what will be covered ahead of time; for example, in a contractual syllabus. They wish to lay out the facts rather than letting an interesting story unfold with its twists and turns.

noted many times that deep learning is like solving a puzzle. Many works of fiction, especially murder mysteries, are based on a surprise twist at the end. The twist makes the story into a puzzle. The puzzle in the murder mystery keeps the reader active and in deep learning mode—the reader is asking him or herself questions to figure out who committed the murder. As with murder mysteries, when a student gets a sudden insight, an epiphany, at the end of a learning activity, it can make a strong impression. Even though the instructor had a plan leading the student to work out the idea, the student gains the impression that he or she constructed it. The insight seems like the student's answer to the student's own question. The idea is more likely to be remembered. There is a greater likelihood of far transfer.

The reader may also remember that this book is designed to be self-reflective. That is, it is organized around the contrarian principles it espouses. Accordingly, there should be a twist at the end of this book. What is the twist? A theme of this book is that learning to be a more insightful and effective learner is an essential goal of a liberal arts and sciences education. Content material covered in a course matters only as a platform to allow students to hone their skills as reflective practitioners ready to apply scholarly-based critical thinking to any issue. From this perspective, it doesn't matter specifically what a student is learning as long as she or he is improving critical thinking skills and learning to become a skilled, mature learner. That is why one gets a similar degree with many completely different majors[79]. The twist is that, in spite of what was stressed earlier, the content of the material in a class or the curriculum does matter. It matters a lot.

The traditional instructor typically asserts that the material learned in a class is the most important aspect of the class. It is literally what the class is about. Traditional instructors warn that we cannot let students learn just anything. Our educational system has the obligation to move students to the most meaningful subjects and the latest research and scholarship. Of course I agree. The curriculum must be comprehensive and it should be built on the traditional disciplines of scholarship stemming from the trivium and the quadrivium. The practical arts are necessary as the society and the economy need universities to provide graduates with skills preparing them to enter all professions. Yet, those traditional perspectives miss the primary point about

---

[79] Some readers may argue about the distinction between a Bachelor of Science and a Bachelor of Arts degree. I agree they are different, but that difference has been eroding. The differences among many majors within either of these degrees is about as large as the contemporary difference between a Bachelor of Science and a Bachelor of Arts degree.

the importance of content material. That is why I didn't stress the importance of content material earlier.

What is the point that these traditional instructors miss? Many times in this book, I have asserted that the central purpose of a college education is not to qualify graduates for a professional job. It is to prepare graduates to lead a more informed life. There are many allusions in the preceding chapters to phrases like: a life of learning, a life that is meaningful, a life contributing to society, or a life directed to sustaining our purposes on Earth. When I have asserted that these phrases are an essential purpose of education, what do I mean? I mean that college has an obligation to help us find and follow passions that provide purpose in life. What do graduates care about most deeply? What differences can they make that champion those ideals? For example, I have a passion for improving the opportunities for deep learning in students' college experience. Writing this book is an effort to further that passion. I have many other passions; e.g., research in the acoustics and physiology of speech production or support for scholarship in general. Those are primary passions related to my professional involvements. I also follow many passions in other parts of my life; like participating in democracy or improving my community. All of us can make long lists of what we care about, what our values are, and what we could promote with our talents and energies. In this regard, I am defining passions as those areas in which we use critical thinking skills and personal commitment to reach out and contribute to our world.

A theme of this book has been that college helps students become better learners. The twist noted above is that college is also a place to find and further ones life passions. Of course, our passions are shaped by many influences like parents and families, culture, friends, experiences, opportunities, individual circumstances, or wild dreams. Students come to college with values. The college experience needs to respect those values, but the curriculum should also lead students to examine their lives and to identify their passions. That is why the curriculum and the material forming the content of any course is essential. College equips students with the learning and leadership tools to make a difference with their lives. The subjects in the curriculum guide them to the passions where they can use those tools to lead and to contribute. That is the twist. The material covered in a class is important to contribute to ones passions.

Unfortunately, not everyone lives a life in which they have examined their values, developed passions, and pursued them. Remember the discussion in Chapter Three about surface, strategic, and deep learning modes? In college, the students in the strategic learning mode are doing what they are told. They pay scant attention to the meaning of the course content in their lives. The concern is that strategic learning does not facilitate the development of passions and a direction in life. If students stay in the strategic learning mode throughout college, then they are likely to do that throughout their later careers and lives. Students who are strategic learners in college become strategic professionals. They don't develop and pursue challenges that are directly meaningful to what they see as a purpose in life. They do what is defined by the system to get ahead. Strategic professionals are motivated to do what will propel them to the top in every external evaluation. As strategic students, these individuals were consumed by chasing extrinsic rewards of points, grades, degrees, and honors. When they graduate and stay in a strategic mode, they continue to be focused primarily on accruing recognized measures of success: high salaries, promotions, positions of power and influence, and accolades of many sorts. Their college experiences equip them to be primarily working the system for extrinsic rewards. They are focused on rewarding themselves, not on making their lives meaningful.

This issue really becomes one about character. Graduates who devote their lives to passions, purposes, and causes are doing so out of a sense of character that goes beyond the personal. These deep learning professionals ask questions about their own purpose and destiny. What should they be doing to make this a better world? They are not asking about what they can do to get ahead; that is, to get an extrinsic reward. They have the character that drives them to contribute to others. In contrast, strategic professionals may have graduated without ever asking what they are trying to accomplish in life. They only know how to climb the professional success ladder. Strategic professionals are inward looking and self-centered; without having learned to be more. One could say that their college instructors have failed them. Or, on the other hand, one could say they have failed themselves. If we blame the students for the students' failure—it is like taking credit for teaching a dog to whistle.

I developed this thought before I read *The Road to Character* by David Brooks (2015), but my concepts comport well with the ideas extolled in that book. Brooks talks about individuals with a sense of character compelling them to pursue passions that will make this a better world. My expectation is that these individuals developed this character through deep learning. Brooks talks about others, I would characterize them as strategic professionals, who are only concerned with climbing the ladder of professional meritocracy. Brooks notes that one can tell the difference by examining how such individuals define the concept of character. Strategic professionals stress character traits useful to get ahead: self-control, grit, resilience, and tenacity. Those with passion centered on deep learning and shaping our world, stress character traits like selflessness, generosity, self-sacrifice, empathy, compassion, and concern for long-term effects of societal actions. These traits may make it less likely for such individuals to get ahead professionally, but they lay the groundwork for living a meaningful life.

This chapter has been about leadership. This latter section is about the role of college in preparing students to know where their efforts at leadership should take them and us. Clearly deep learning in college helps prepare our graduates to be effective leaders. It also helps graduates examine themselves and build character traits and personal skills instrumental in successful leadership. The content of our courses helps students connect the skills they are developing with real-world issues that they can pursue. Content is vitally important as it informs us, as leaders, about where we can and should be going in life--where we should lead. Learning and leading tools are only important because of what one can do with them.

Chapter 14

CONCLUSION:
ASKING THE RIGHT QUESTIONS

Deep learners thrive on asking their own questions. As you have been reading this book, I hope you have been formulating your own questions about the contrarian ideas presented. Maybe you have heard many of them before. They are not new and most of the ideas are being used and developed by a growing number of instructors around the world. But raising these issues should lead deep-learning instructors to a number of questions; such as, whether or not the ideas offered will lead to improvements over the traditional approach of organizing college classes around content-rich lectures. In the spirit of Browne & Keeley's (2014) classic book on critical thinking, *Asking the Right Questions*, we should apply the approach to ourselves and ask: Are we asking the right questions?

We can summarize by going over the six interrogative *wh*-words kids often learn in grade school: what, when, where, who, why, and how.

- **What?** For students to learn deeply, they need to think about material and analyze it. They need structured reflective practice to learn to apply their critical thinking skills, to form their own questions, to seek their own answers, and to express and justify their conclusions to others. They need content material as a foundation for their questions, but not much, and generally much less than one typically finds in a lecture or a course as a whole. Content is there to help formulate the passions they will pursue throughout their lives.
- **When?** In the traditional approach, new content is provided in lectures and students are expected to study the material outside of

class. The contrarian approach flips the classroom. Classroom time is most valuable because of the face-to-face interaction the students have with the instructor and each other. Instructors can use class time to stimulate thinking activities, such as questioning each other, analyzing their ideas, and searching together for answers. It is not necessary to waste much classroom time presenting new material when it can be introduced outside of class, especially with today's capacity for creating many different types of polished and provocative presentations online. Classroom time can be effective for oral testing, but for the most part written testing can be done online outside of class.

- **Where?** Classrooms are a valuable resource for getting students to interact with each other and the instructor and to stimulate and support each other's questioning. Instructors should be an active participant in ensuring that the physical structure of the classroom facilitates interaction. The content of our courses also directs students to insights about where they can focus the passions of their lives. As good critical thinkers are equipped and motivated to lead others, course content can help them decide where to lead them.

- **Who?** It is not expected that every instructor will ascribe to the contrarian practices advocated. Lecturing does work, especially if students develop the abilities to be deep learners through other means. However, the number of instructors using such techniques as the flipped classroom and active discussion in class has been growing steadily. When instructors stimulate deep learning, students ask probing questions that generate exciting ideas and motivate both students and instructors. The instructors learn more when teaching this way. One might also assert that the "who" in this question should refer to students as well as instructors. With deep learning the student is taking more of the responsibility for guiding his or her learning, for stimulating such learning in other students, and preparing to be a leader.

- **Why?** Students begin college with very different ideas about why they are there from those of instructors. Students have a number of misconceptions about how to learn effectively and they spend too much time with surface and strategic learning activities. Students need to be guided to develop critical thinking skills that will lead to deep learning and the desire to ask ones own questions. As instructors, we must direct our focus away from teaching based on how clear, organized, or entertaining it might be; to a more explicit concern for what the students are learning. Deep learning is what really matters, it leads to far transfer of material, and it has the most potential to equip our students to lead meaningful lives.

- **How?** There are many ways to design the educational experience to promote reflective practice that fosters the development of deep learning. These include involving students in research activities, internships, and clinical practicums of all sort. One can teach critical thinking explicitly and point out misunderstandings about how we learn. As mentioned above, one of the important tools is to flip the classroom to foster student interaction and questioning.

As an ending comment, I have a admonition that relates to the "how" question. Instructors should be selective as they choose ideas from material in this book and in the literature on deep learning. What works for one instructor may not work so well for someone else. The contrarian perspective asserts that the more you are different from your students, the more impact your genuine approach will have as it will broaden them. Share your uniqueness and let it guide students in developing their own questions, testing them, and acting on their findings. Most importantly, be yourself. There is nothing more real, more inspiring, than being an eloquent spokesperson for a background, a culture, or a way of life that is genuine. Although critical thinking is important, it doesn't have nearly as much influence in our society as lovable symbols inspired by personal contact with people who value them.

REFERENCES

Aldrich, C. (2009). *The complete guide to simulations & serious games.* San Francisco: Pfeiffer.

Alfieri, L., Brooks, P. J., Aldrich, N. J., & Tenenbaum, H. R. (2011). Does discovery-based instruction enhance learning? *Journal of Educational Psychology*, 103(1), 1-18.

Ambrose, S. A., Bridges, M. W., Lovett, M. C. DiPietro, M, & Norman, M. K. (2010). *How learning works: Seven research-based principles for smart teaching,* San Francisco: Jossey-Bass.

American Academy of Arts and Sciences (2013). *The heart of the matter.* Cambridge MA: Retrieved from www.amacad.org.

Arum, R. & Roksa, J. (2010). *Academically adrift: Limited learning on college campuses.* Chicago: University of Chicago Press.

Bain, K. (2012). *What the best college students do.* Cambridge, MA: Harvard University Press.

Barr, R. B. & Tagg, J. (1995). From teaching to learning: A new paradigm for undergraduate education. *Change*, 27, 12-25.

Barlett, F. C. (1932). *Remembering: A study in experimental and social psychology,* London: Cambridge University Press.

Barkley, E. F. (2010). *Student engagement techniques: A handbook for college faculty.* San Francisco: Jossey-Bass.

Beck, J. C. & Wade, M. (2004). *Got game: How the gamer generation is reshaping business forever.* Boston MA: Harvard Business School Press.

Best, J. (2006). *Flavor of the month: Why smart people fall for fads.* Berkeley: University of California Press.

Benassi, V. A., Overson, C. E., & Hakala, C. M. (2014). *Applying science of learning in education: Infusing psychological science into the curriculum.* Washington DC: American Psychological Association.

Bennett, W. J. & Wilezol, D. (2013). *Is college worth it?: A former United States Secretary of Education and a liberal arts graduate expose the broken promise of higher education.* Nashville: Thomas Nelson.

Bereiter, C. & Scardamalia, M. (2005). Beyond Bloom's taxonomy: Rethinking knowledge for the knowledge age, In Fullan M. (Ed), *Fundamental Change*, 5.22.

Bloom, A. (1987). *The closing of the American mind.* New York: Simon & Schuster. Bloom, B. (1984). The 2 sigma problem: The search for methods of group instruction as effective as one-on-one tutoring. *Educational Researcher*, 13(6), 4-16.

Bok, D. (2006). *Our underachieving colleges: A candid look at how much students learn and why they should be learning more.* Princeton NJ: Princeton University Press.

Bogue, E. G. & Aper, J. (2000). *Exploring the heritage of American higher education: The evolution of philosophy and policy.* Phoenix: ACE/Orix Press.

Boud, D. & Walker, D. (1998). Promoting reflection in professional courses: The challenge of context. *Studies in Higher Education*, 23(2), 191-206.

Boyer, E. L. (1990). *Scholarship reconsidered: Priorities of the professoriate.* New York: Carnegie Foundation for the Advancement of Teaching and John Wiley & Sons.

Brackenbury, T., Folkins, J. W., & Ginsberg, S. M. (2014). Examining educational challenges in communication sciences and disorders from the perspectives of signature pedagogy and reflective practice. *Contemporary Issues in Communication Science and Disorders*, 41, 70-82.

Brooks, D. (2015). *The road to character.* New York: Random House.

Brooks, D. C. (2012). Space and consequences: The impact of different formal learning spaces on instructor and student behavior. *Journal of Learning Spaces*, 1(2).

Brown, P. C., Roediger, H. L. & McDaniel, M. A. (2014). *Make it stick: The science of successful learning.* Cambridge MA: The Belknap Press of Harvard University Press.

Browne, M. N., Keeley, S. M. (2014). *Asking the right questions*, 11th ed., Boston: Pearson.

Burns, J. M. (1978). *Transforming leadership.* New York: Grove Press.

Bush, V. (1945). *Science—The endless frontier: A report to the President on a program for postwar scientific research*, Washington, DC: National Science Foundation, reprinted 1990.

Calzonetti, F. J. (2003). Navigating local economic development expectations at an emerging research university: Raising academic stature vs. rapid local returns, *Journal for Higher Education Strategists*, 1(1), 33-50.

Carey, B. (2014). *How we learn: The surprising truth about when, where, and why it happens.* New York: Random House.

Carolla, A. (2009). Slippery slope guy. Available from youtube.com.

Chatfield, T. (2010). *Fun Inc.: Why gaming will dominate the twenty-first century.* New York: Pegasus Books.

Chew, S. L. (2014). Helping students to get the most out of studying. In Barnassi, V. A., Overson, C. E. & Hakala, C. M. (Eds.). *Appling science of learning to education.* Society for the Teaching of Psychology. Retrieved from www.google.com/url?url=http://teachpsych.org/Resources/Documents/ebooks/asle2014.pdf&rct=j&frm=1&q=&esrc=s&sa=U&ei=74e9U8ubFcGOyAT66oLACA&ved=0CBwQFjAB&usg=AFQjCNHWJ7fdJ6DSw0p3TjxkaxxImrkFHg.

Coby, A., Ehrlich, T., Beaumont, E. & Stephens, J. (2003). Educating citizens: Preparing America's graduates for lives of moral and civic responsibility. San Francisco: Jossey-Bass.

Concerned Children's Advertisers (1999). *North American House Hippo.* Available at (https://search.yahoo.com/search?fr=mcafee&type=C211US676D20151207&p=house+hippo).

Collins, J. & Porras, J. I. (1994). *Built to last: Successful habits of visionary companies.* New York: Harper Business.

Cook, J. & Lewandowsky, S. (2011). *The debunking handbook.* St Lucia, Australia: University of Queensland, http://sks.to/debunk.

Council on Undergraduate Research, http://www.cur.org/.

Crandell, C. & Smalldino, J. (1995). The importance of room acoustics. In: *Assistive devices for persons with hearing impairment*, eds., R. S. Tyler & D. Schum, Needham Heights MA: Allyn and Bacon, 142-164.

Damer, T. E. (2005). *Attacking faulty reasoning: A practical guide to fallacy-free arguments*, 5th edition. Belmont, CA: Thompson-Wadsworth.

Dawkins, R. (2011). *The magic of reality: How we know what's really true.* New York: Free Press

DeAngelo, L., Hurtado, S., Pryor, J. H., Kelly, K. R. & J. L. Santos, J. L (2009). *The American College Teacher: National Norms for the 2007–*

2008 HERI Faculty Survey. Los Angeles: Higher Education Research Institute, University of California–Los Angeles.

Denning, S. (2007). *The secret language of leadership: How leaders inspire action through narrative.* San Francisco: Jossey-Bass.

DePree, M. (1989). *Leadership is an art.* New York: Doubleday.

Dewey, J. (1910). *How we think.* Boston: Haughton-Mifflin.

Dollaghan, C. A. (2007). *The handbook for evidence-based practice in communication disorders.* Baltimore, MD: Brookes.

Driscoll, D. L. (2014). Clashing values: A longitudinal, exploratory study of student beliefs about general education, vocationalism, and transfer of learning. *Teaching & Learning Inquiry,* 2 (1), 21-37.

Edmundson, M. (1997). On the uses of a liberal education I: As the entertainment of bored college students. *Harper's Magazine.* September 1 issue.

Einstein, A. (1954). *Ideas and opinions.* New York: Three Rivers Press.

Elgren, T., & Hensel, N. (2006). Undergraduate research experiences: Synergies between scholarship and teaching. *Association of American Colleges & Universities,* 4-7.

Elliott, E. S. & Dweck, C. S. (1988). Goals: An approach to motivation and achievement. *Journal of Personality and Social Psychology.* 54(1), 5-12.

Entertainment Software Association (2014). Industry facts. Retrieved from http://www.theesa.com/facts/gameplayer.asp.

Entwistle, N. (1984). Contrasting perspectives on learning. In F. Marton, D. Hounsell, & N. Entwistle, *The experience of learning,* Edinburgh: Scottish Academic Press, 1-18.

Ferrall, V. E. (2011). *Liberal arts at the brink.* Cambridge: Harvard University Press.

Finn, P. (2014). A model of critical thinking for the helping professions, ASHA convention presentation, session 1430.

Finn, P., Brundage, S. B., & DiLollo, A. (2016). Preparing our future helping professionals to become critical thinkers: A tutorial. *Perspectives of the ASHA Special Interest Groups,* SIG 10, 1(2), 1-25.

Firestein, S. (2012). *Ignorance: How it drives science.* Oxford, England: Oxford University Press.

Florida, R. (2000). *The rise of the creative class: And how it's transforming work, leisure, community, and everyday life.* New York: Basic Books.

Folkins, J. W. (2010). Redesigning introduction to communication disorders, *Perspectives on Issues in Higher Education,* 13(2), 1-14.

Folkins, J. W. (2011). Perspectives on the teaching of pedagogy to doctoral students. *Perspectives on Issues in Higher Education*, 14(2), 57-63.

Folkins, J. W. (2016). Are We Asking the Right Questions about Pedagogy in Communication Sciences and Disorders? *Current Issues in Communication Sciences and Disorders*, 43, 77-86, 2016.

Folkins, J. W., Friberg, J. C. & Cesarini, P. A. (2015). University classroom design principles to facilitate learning—The instructor as advocate, *Planning for Higher Education*, 43(2), 45-62.

Folkins, J. W., Brackenbury, T., Krause, M., and Haviland, A. (2016). Enhancing the therapy experience using principles of video game design, *American Journal of Speech-Language Pathology*, 25, 111-121.

Forni, P. M. (2011). *The thinking life: How to thrive in the age of distraction.* New York: St. Martin's Griffin.

Freedman, J. O. (2003). *Liberal education & the public interest.* Iowa City: University of Iowa Press.

Freeman, S., Eddy, S. L., McDonough, M., Smith, M. K., Okoroafor, N., Jordt, H., & Wenderoth, M. P. (2014). Active learning increases student performance in science, engineering, and mathematics. *Proceedings of the National Academy of Sciences*, 111(23), 8410-8415.

Friberg, J. C., Folkins, J. W., & Visconti, C. F. (2013). Using clinical and research activities to enhance the undergraduate experience, *Perspectives on Issues in Higher Education*, 16(2), 81-85.

Gee, J. P. (2007). *What video games have to teach us about learning and literacy*, revised and updated edition. New York: Palgrave McMillan.

Gilovich, T. (1991). *How we know what isn't so: The fallibility of human reason in everyday life.* New York: Free Press.

Ginsberg, S. M., Friberg, J. C., & Visconti, C. F. (2012). *Scholarship of teaching and learning in speech-language pathology and audiology.* San Diego: Plural Publishing.

Glaze, J. (2001). Reflection as a transforming process: Student advanced nurse practitioners' experiences of developing reflective skills as part of an MSc Programme. *Journal of Advanced Nursing*, 34(5), 639-647.

Gleitman, H., Gross, J., & Reisberg, D. (2011). *Psychology*, 8th edition. New York: W.W. Norton.

Goldson, E. (2010). Valedictory Speech, Coxsackie-Athens High School. Athens, NY. Retrieved from americaviaerica.blogspot.com/2010/07/coxsackie-athens-valedictorian-speech.html.

Gottlieb, A. (2016). *The dream of enlightenment: The rise of modern philosophy.* New York: Liveright Publishing Corporation.

Grunert O'Brien, J. G., Mills, B. J., & Cohan, M. W. (2008). *The course syllabus: A learning-centered approach* (2nd ed.), San Francisco: Jossey-Bass.

Gula, R. J. (2007). *Nonsense: Red herrings, straw men and sacred cows: How we abuse logic in our everyday language.* Mount Jackson VA: Axios Press.

Gumprecht, B. (2008). *The American college town.* Amhurst: University of Massachusetts Press.

Harkavy, I., & Hartley, M. (2008). Pursuing Franklins' democratic vision for higher education, *Peer Review*, 10(2), 13-17.

Harris, M. S. (2006). Out out, damned spot: General education in a market-driven institution. *The Journal of General Education,* 55(3), 186-200.

Harris poll (2013). http://www.theharrispoll.com/health-and-life/Americans__ Belief_ in_God__Miracles_and_Heaven_Declines.html).

Haskins, C. H. (1923). *The rise of universities.* Ithaca: Cornell University Press.

Hay, D. B., Williams, D., Stahl, D. & Wingate, R. J. (2013). Using drawings of the brain cell to exhibit expertise in neuroscience: Exploring the boundaries of experimental culture. *Science Education,* 97(3), 468-491.

Hattery, A. J. (2003). Sleeping in the box, thinking outside the box: Student reflections on innovative pedagogical tools for teaching about and promoting a greater understanding of social class inequality among undergraduates, *Teaching Sociology*, 31, 412-427.

Heffernan. M. (2011). *Willful blindness: Why we ignore the obvious at our peril.* New York: Bloomsbury Publishing.

Hertz, N. (2010). How to use experts—and when not to, TED talk, London, November. Retrieved from http://www.ted.com/talks/noreena_ hertz_how_to_use_experts_and_when_not_to.

Hertzog, J. & Williams, R. (2007). Applying sociology through social marketing: Student reflections on an intimate violence awareness project, *Teaching Sociology*, 35, 166-173.

Hersh, R. H., & Merrow, J. (2005). *Declining by degrees: Higher education at risk.* New York: Palgrave Macmillan.

Hill, M. C. & Epps, K. K. (2010). The impact of physical classroom environment on student satisfaction and student evaluation of teaching in the university environment. *Academy of Educational Leadership Journal,* 14(4), 65-79.

Hofstadter, D. R. (1985). *Metamagical themas: Questing for the essence of mind and pattern,* Section I: Snags and Snarls. New York: Basic Books.

Isaacson, W. (2003). *Benjamin Franklin: An American life*. New York: Simon & Schuster.

Johnson, W. (1946). *People in quandaries: The semantics of personal adjustment*. New York: Harper & Row.

Kahneman, D. (2011). *Thinking fast and slow*. New York: Farrar, Straus, Giroux.

Kanter, R. M. (2004). *Confidence: How winning streaks and losing streaks begin and end*. New York: Crown Publishing Group.

Kapp, K. M. (2012). *The gamification of learning and instruction: Game-based methods and strategies for training and education*. San Francisco: John Wiley & Sons.

Kardash, C. (2000). Evaluation of undergraduate research experiences: Perceptions of undergraduate interns and their faculty mentors. *Journal of Educational Psychology*, 92, 191-201.

Kernan, A. (1999). *In Plato's cave*. New Haven: Yale University Press.

Kida, T. (2006). *Don't believe everything you think: The 6 basic mistakes we make in thinking*. Amherst NY: Prometheus Books.

Knight, W. E., Folkins, J. W., Hakel, M. D., & Kennell, R. P. (2011). Administrators' decisions about resource allocation. *Journal of Higher Education Policy and Management*, 33, 325-336.

Knewton, Inc. (2014). The gamification of education infographic. Retrieved from http://www.knewton.com/gamification-education/.

Komives, S. R., Lucas, N., & McMahon, T. R. (2007). *Exploring leadership*, 2nd Ed., San Francisco: John Wiley & Sons.

Koper, R. (2014). Conditions for effective smart learning environments. *Smart Learning Environments*, 1(5), 1-20.

Koster, R. (2005). *A theory of fun for game design*. Sebastopol, CA: O'Reilly Media.

Kouzes, J. M. & Posner, B. Z. (2012). *The leadership challenge*, 5th Ed., San Francisco: Jossey-Bass.

Krathwohl, D. R. (2002). A revision of Bloom's taxonomy: An overview, *Theory into Practice*, 41(4), 212-218.

Krugman, P. (2015). Hating good government, *The New York Times,* Opinion Pages, January 19, http://nyti.mx/1KUpFSh.

Kuh, G. D., Schuh, J. H., Whitt, E. J., & Associates (1991). *Involving colleges: Successful approaches to fostering student and personal development and student learning outside the classroom*. San Francisco: Jossey-Bass.

Kuh, G. D., Kinzie, J., Schuh, J. H., Whitt, E. J., & Associates (2005). *Student success in college: Creating conditions that matter.* San Francisco: Jossey-Bass.

Lang, J. M. (2013). Why don't they apply what they've learned? *The Chronicle of Higher Education,* Part I January 2013, Part II February 2013, Part III March 2013. Washington D.C.

Lecky-Thompson, G. W. (2007). *Video game design revealed.* Boston, MA: Cengage Learning.

Levetin, D. J. (2016). Identifying Expertise, In: *A field guide to lies,* New York: Dutton, 129-151.

Ludy, M-J., Brackenbury T. Folkins, J. W., Peet, S., Langendorfer, S. J., & Beining, K. (2016). Student impressions of syllabus design: Engaging versus contractual syllabus. *International Journal for the Scholarship of Teaching and Learning,* 10(2), 1-23.

Machiavelli, N. (2014). *The prince.* Narragansett, RI: Millennium Publications.

Mackay, A. I. (1977). *The harvest of a quiet eye: A selection of scientific quotations.* New York: Crane, Russak & Company, Inc.

Mangels, J. A., Butterfield, B., Lamb, J., Good, C, & Dweck, C. S. (2006). Why do beliefs about intelligence influence learning success? A social cognitive neuroscience model. *SCAN,* 1, 75-86.

Mann, J., Gordon, J., & MacLeod, A. (2009). Reflection and reflective practice in health professions education: A systematic review. *Advances in Health Sciences Education, Theory and Practice.* 14, 595-621.

Manrique, V. (2013). Why people play: Games and human motivators. Epic Win Blog. [web log post]. Retrieved from http://www.epicwinblog.net/2013/06/the-35-gamification-mechanics-toolkit.html.

Marton, F. & Booth, S. (1997). *Learning and awareness.* New York: Routledge.

Marton, F., Hounsell, D., & Entwistle, N. J. (1997). *The experience of learning,* 2nd Edition. Edinburgh: Scottish Academic Press.

Marton, F. & Säljö, R. (1976). On qualitative differences in learning: I outcome and process, *British Journal of Educational Psychology,* 46, 4-11.

Massey, W. F. (2003). *Honoring the trust: Quality and cost containment in higher education.* Bolton, MA: Anker Publishing.

Matekca, K., & Kurke, L. B. (2004). Designing a great syllabus. *College Teaching,* 42(3), 115-117.

McGonigal, J. (2011). *Reality is broken: Why games make us better and how they can change the world*. New York: The Penguin Press.

McKeachie, W. J. & Svinicki, M. (2013). *McKeachie's teaching tips: Strategies, research, and strategy for college and university teachers*, 14th edition. Belmont CA: Wadsworth.

Michaelson, L. K., Bauman-Knight, A. & Fink, L. D. (2003). *Team-based learning: A transformative use of small groups in college teaching*. Westport, CT: Praeger.

Mojang (2011). *Minecraft*. Stockholm, Sweden: Mojang.

Moon, J. (2004). *A handbook of reflective and experimental learning: Theory and practice*. London: Routledge Farmer.

Newstock, S. L. (2014). A plea for "close learning." Blog posting, February 20. Stanford Center for Teaching and Learning. Retrieved from https://teachingcommonsstanford.edu/teaching-talk/case-close-learning.

Nilson, L. B. (2007). *Teaching at its best: A research-based resource for college instructors*. San Francisco: Jossey-Bass.

Nintendo EAD (1985). *Super Mario Bros*. Kyoto, Japan: Nintendo

Noddings, N. (2013). Renewing the spirit of the liberal arts. *Journal of General Education*, 62(2), 77-83.

Northouse, P. G. (2013). *Leadership: Theory and practice*, 6th Ed. Los Angeles: Sage.

Oblinger, D. (2003). Boomers, gen-Xers, & millennials: Understanding the new students. *Educause Review*, July/August 37-47.

Oppong, S. (2013). Should higher education institutions serve national economic needs? Why and why not. *Education Sciences & Psychology*, 25(3), 90-109.

Oreskes, N. & Conway, E. (2011). *Merchants of doubt: How a handful of scientists obscured the truth on issues from tobacco smoke to global warming*. New York: Bloomsbury Publishing.

Pascarella, E. T. & Terenzini, P. T. (2005). *How college affects students, volume 2, A third decade of research*. San Francisco: Jossey-Bass.

Paul, A. M. (2016). The future of the professor, and more. *The Brilliant Report* (blog), May. Retrieved from http://anniemurphypaul. com/2016/05/the-future-of-the-professor/

Pintrich, P. R., & Garcia, T. (1991). Student goal orientation and self-regulation in the college classroom. In Maehr, M. & Pintrich. P. R. (Eds.), *Advances in motivation and achievement: Goals and self-regulatory processes*, 7, 371-402, Greenwich, CT: JAI Press.

Peligiri, J. (2012). Universities reach out to males for study abroad. *The GW Hatchet*, March 1, retrieved from http://www.gwhatchet.com/2012/03/01/universities-reach-out-to-males-for-study-abroad-3/.

Poovey, M. (1998). *A history of the modern fact*. Chicago: The University of Chicago Press.

Poulter, P. J. (1994). Disciplinary society and the myth of aesthetic justice. In: Scheer, B. C. & Preiser, W. F. E. (Eds.), *Design review: Challenging urban aesthetics control*, New York: Chapman & Hall, 175-186.

Pryor, J. H., Eagan, K., Palucki Blake, L., Hurtado, S., Berdan, J., & Case, M. H. (2012). *The American freshman: National norms fall 2012*. Los Angeles: Higher Education Research Institute, UCLA.

Provine, R. R. (2012). *Curious behavior: Yawning, laughing, hiccupping, and beyond*. Cambridge MA: Belknap Press of Harvard University Press.

Robbin, E. D. (1973). The evolutionary advantages of being stupid, *Perspectives in Biology and Medicine, 16*(3), 369-380.

Rogers, S. (2010). *Level up!: The guide to great video game design*. West Sussex, UK: John Wiley & Sons.

Roth, M. S. (2014). *Beyond the university: Why liberal education matters*. New Haven: Yale University Press.

Russell, S., Hancock, M., & McCullough, J. (2007). Benefits of undergraduate research experiences. *Science, 316*, 548-549.

Ryan, R & Deci, E. (2000). When rewards compete with nature: The undermining of intrinsic motivation and self-regulation. In Sansone, C. & Harackiewics, J. (Eds.), *Intrinsic and extrinsic motivation: The search for optimal motivation and performance*. San Diego: Academic Press.

Sample, S. B. (2002). *The contrarian's guide to leadership*. San Francisco: Jossey-Bass.

Sanbonmatsu, D. M., Strayer, D. L, Medeiros-Ward, N., & Watson, J M. (2013). Who multi-tasks and why? Multi-tasking ability, perceived multi-tasking ability, impulsivity, and sensation seeking. *PLoS One, 8*, 1-8.

Sawyer, E. (2013). Learning spaces and 21st century skills. *Creativity & Innovation* (blog), January 22. Retrieved from http://tcpd.org/Thornbrg/Handouts/Campfires.pdf.

Schell, J. (2008). *The art of game design: A book of lenses*. Burlington MA: Elsevier.

Schneider, C. G. & Humphries, D. (2005). Putting liberal education on the radar screen. Point of view, *The Chronicle of Higher Education*, B20.

Schön, D. A. (1983). *The reflective practitioner: How professionals think in action*. London: Maurice Temple Smith Ltd.

Schön, D. A. (1987). *Educating the reflective practitioner: Toward a new design for teaching and learning in the professions*. San Francisco: Jossey-Bass.

Scott, A. O. (2016). *Better living through criticism: How to think about art, pleasure, beauty, and truth*. New York: Penguin Press.

Searchquotes (2017). Retrieved from http://www.searchquotes.com/search/ Womens_Education/3/.

Selingo, J. J. (2013). *College (un)bound: The future of higher education and what it means for students*. Boston: Haughton, Mifflin, Harcourt.

Shaffer, D. W., Squire, K. R., Halverson, R. & Gee, J. P. (2005). Video games and the future of learning. *WCER Working Paper*. No. 2005-4. Retrieved from http://www.wcer.wisc.edu/.

Shapiro, H. T. (2005). *A larger sense of purpose: Higher education and society*. Princeton, N.J.: Princeton University Press.

Shapiro, J. (2015). Nine facts about video games and the people who play them. *Forbes*, retrieved from http://www.forbes.com/sites/ jordanshapiro /2015/12/18/9-facts-about-video-games-and-the-people-who-play-them-from-pews-new-study/#33b5eda75ad7.

Shermer, M. (2011). *The believing brain: From ghosts and gods to politics and conspiracies—How we construct beliefs and reinforce them as truths*. New York: Henry Holt and Company.

Shulman, L. S. (2005). Signature pedagogies in the professions. *Daedalus*, 134, 52-59.

Shute, V. J. (2008). Focus on formative feedback. *Review of Educational Research*, 78(1), 153-189.

Smith, R. V, (2006). *Where you stand is where you sit: An academic administrator's handbook*. Fayetteville: The University of Arkansas Press.

Sood, S. (2012). The statistics of studying abroad. *The British Broadcasting Company*, September 26. Retrieved from http://www.bbc. com/ travel/story/20120926-the-statistics-of-studying-abroad.

Squire, R. (2011). *Video games and learning: Teaching and participatory culture in the digital age*. New York: Teachers College Press.

Stanovich, K. (2009). *What intelligence tests miss*. New Haven: Yale.

Stoll, C. (1999). *High-tech heretic: Why computers don't belong in the classroom and other reflections by a computer contrarian*. New York: Doubleday.

Sun Tzu (2015). *The art of war*. Wisehouse, Sweden: Chiron Academic Press.

Tavris, C. & Aronson, E. (2007). *Mistakes were made (but not by me): Why we justify foolish beliefs, bad decisions, and hurtful acts.* New York: Harcourt, Inc.

The Paper Chase, (1973). See https://en.wikipedia.org/wiki/The_ Paper _Chase_(film).

Titze, I. R. (2010). *Fascinations with the human voice.* Salt Lake City UT: National Center for Voice and Speech.

Truss, L. (2003). *Eats, shoots & leaves: The zero tolerance approach to punctuation.* New York: Gotham Books.

Vygotsky, L. S. (1978). *Mind and society: The development of higher psychological processes.* Cambridge, MA: Harvard University Press.

Waitzkin, J. (2007). *The art of learning.* New York: Free Press.

Walker, J. D., Brooks, D. C., & Baepler, P. (2011). Pedagogy and space: Empirical research on new learning environments. *EDUCAUSE Quarterly,* 34(4).

Wegner, E. (1998). *Communities of practice: Learning, meaning, and identity.* Cambridge: Cambridge University Press.

Weimer, M. (2002). *Learner-centered teaching: Five key changes to practice.* San Francisco: Jossey-Bass.

Willingham, D. T. (2009). *Why don't students like school? A cognitive scientist answers questions about how the mind works and what it means for the classroom.* San Francisco: Jossey-Bass.

Young, R. B. (1997). *No neutral ground: Standing by the values we prize in higher education.* San Francisco: Jossey-Bass.

Zakaria, F. (2015). *In defense of liberal education.* New York: W. W. Norton.

Zander, R. S. & Zander, B. (2002). *The art of possibility: Transforming professional and personal life.* New York: Penguin Random House.

Zen Pencil, (2013). *I'm Graduating.* Retrieved from http://zenpencils. com/comic/123-erica-goldson-graduation-speech.

ACKNOWLEDGMENTS

I continue to learn from the insights of colleagues and students. I thank them all. I am especially grateful to the individuals who went out of their way to provide sage advice on preliminary drafts of this manuscript: Paul A. Moore, M. Neil Browne, Jenifer C. Friberg, Rosalind R. Scudder, Pete L. Trotter, Ronald W. Johnson, Patrick Finn, Pollyanna E. F. Hampton, and Claire V. Zois. I also wish to thank my wife, Georgianna, for putting up with me while I was preparing this manuscript.

I owe a debt to all of the authors who are cited; however, there are some who were especially inspirational: Steven B. Sample for his use of the contrarian approach; Ference Marton, Dai Hounsell, and Noel Entwistle for developing ideas about surface, strategic, and deep learning; Donald Schön for promoting reflective practice; M. Neil Browne for emphasizing the role of asking questions in critical thinking; John Cooke and Stephen Lewandowsky for offering techniques to debunk myths; Daniel T. Willingham for insights from experimental psychology about learning; James Paul Gee for ideas about how video games can guide educational practice; and David Brooks for his emphasis on leadership that serves others.

ABOUT THE AUTHOR

John Wm. Folkins, Ph.D.
Provost and Vice President for Academic Affairs Emeritus,
Bowling Green State University

I never intended to write this book. Some people lead lives that are directed. They make strategic plans early and work directly to achieve them. My career wasn't like that. My strategic directions changed, often at unexpected junctures. The result is that the twists and turns provided an array of academic experiences that seemed somewhat disconnected at the time. I now realize that this circuitous background has uniquely motivated and informed me to write this book. These experiences fit together well to make points that are informed by personal experience.

I have sometimes remarked that I have held positions representative of every general area of academia: student, staff member, faculty member, and administrator. I have sampled many discipline areas, programs, and levels of responsibility:

- I was a student for ten years. At the University of Redlands, which is a small independent liberal arts university, I changed my major three times. Following a master's degree at the University of Redlands, I ended up in speech science which is also called experimental phonetics. As it is a blend of acoustics, physiology, psychology, and phonetics; it spans the physical sciences, social sciences, and humanities. It provides some of the theoretical and experimental support for the work of speech-language pathologists, thus there are clinical and interprofessional experiences in my background. After five years as a doctoral student in speech science at the University of Washington, which is a large research-based state university, I spent another year at the University of Washington as a postdoctoral researcher in the Departments of Orthodontics and Physiology & Biophysics.

- In 1977, I began as a faculty member at the University of Iowa. For the first nine years, I was consumed by research and supporting a series of research grants from the National Institutes of Health and the National Science Foundation. I taught regularly during this time, but my emphasis was with graduate teaching. I especially wanted to groom doctoral students to embrace my theoretical perspectives and to carry on similar lines of research. I wanted them to think like me and to have values like mine. Undergraduate teaching was a responsibility that I accepted as a necessary distraction. I liked it, but I had a full plate and there was always a struggle to keep the research support to fund the close-knit team in the laboratory. During this time, much of my teaching was in providing scientific background to undergraduate majors in speech-language pathology and audiology. These students wanted to learn the skills to be a clinicians. Often they didn't see the need to learn about science or to care about the theory and evidence underlying their future clinical activities. When I think back on it, at that time I was very traditional in my approach to teaching. I thought the job of an instructor was to cover material clearly and comprehensively. If one interjected some jokes in a lecture, that was good even if the jokes might have been off topic and distracting. At least the instructor was entertaining. I was among the last professors one might imagine writing the present book. The one exception to my preoccupation with research was my experience teaching an introductory class surveying the disciplines of speech-language pathology and audiology. I realized early the power of introductory courses.

- In 1985, I became Chair of the Department of Communication Sciences and Disorders at the University of Iowa. This is one of the oldest and largest departments preparing speech-language pathologists and audiologists in the country. I soon became immersed in many administrative duties, including faculty assessment, strategic planning, and curricular issues for both undergraduate and graduate programs. In addition to continuing research and teaching, I expanded national service activities such as editing two scholarly journals and serving on the Advisory Council for one of the National Institutes of Health: The National Institute on Deafness and Other Communication Disorders. In 1992, as a representative of this Council, I served on a strategic planning task-force for the entire National Institutes of Health, thus advising federal funding for medical research across the country.

- In 1993, I began as an Associate Provost at the University of Iowa[80]. In my first years as Associate Provost, I focused on strategic planning, accountability, and reaccreditation. Later the focus shifted more to undergraduate education. However, throughout this time I dealt with curriculum design; innovative teaching and learning; influences of technology on teaching; classroom design; and student support services including the offices of the Registrar, Admissions, Financial Aid, Student Evaluation and Testing, and Undergraduate Academic Advising. I attended Faculty Senate meetings, served on the Board in Control of Athletics, acted as the Library Liaison to central administration, and was a reviewer for the University of Iowa Press. I was active with national groups promoting technology in college teaching, such as Educause and the National Learning Infrastructure Initiative. It took a few years, but my interests and passions changed from research in speech production to innovations, not just in teaching, but to the entire learning experience of students.

- In 2000, I became Provost at Bowling Green State University. For seven years, I dealt with the wide variety of academic issues one would expect the provost of a research-based state university to handle. Much of the focus related to faculty support and welfare as we had 850 to 900 faculty members. Bowling Green State University is a large institution and there were initiatives in many areas, some were

---

[80] Let me explain what an Associate Provost is: Universities have a President, who focuses a lot on representing the institution to constituent groups and especially to the trustees. The President is also responsible for the operation of the university and, especially in large institutions, the President will work closely with the Vice Presidents. There are typically four to six Vice Presidents who are assigned to different divisions of the University, such as student affairs, financial management, or the physical plant. The President sets a general course and the Vice Presidents lead their constituents to follow that course. The Provost is the Vice President responsible for the academic areas of the university including all of the teaching and research. Faculty connect to the Provost as follows: Faculty members are all assigned to departments. All of the department Chairs report to the Deans of their college. All of the college Deans report to the Provost. Provosts typically have a number of Associate (or Vice) Provosts who are assigned to help lead initiatives in various areas, like undergraduate education, faculty issues, strategic planning, or special initiatives.

similar to the work done at the University of Iowa, but as Provost instead of Associate Provost, the domain was expanded. Through the years, my passion became more and more directed to improving student learning and faculty research.

- In 2007 I left the position of Provost and became the founding Chief Executive Officer of a new nonprofit company that was owned by the University, the *Bowling Green State University Research Institute*. Its mission was to find innovative work done by the faculty, such as: ideas that were patentable, work that was copyrightable, or faculty know-how; and then to work with business and industry to develop new products and services. Many of these projects involved innovative teaching materials. I was chosen because of how well I knew the faculty members and their values. I could convince professors to step from the laboratory long enough to promote their work. This emphasis of the BGSU Research Institute on engagement between researchers and the business community was a great example of how engagement with the community can be a valuable learning experience for students. I continued in this position for two years as the company got started.

- From 2009 to 2015, I served as a full-time faculty member. This was the first time since 1985 I had had full-time faculty responsibilities. I loved it. In addition to teaching, I served on national committees and boards. I also served the University in a number of ways, including being elected as Chair of the Faculty Senate[81] and receiving the University's Distinguished Service Award. During this time, I developed a program of scholarly research about innovative teaching. It was based on my years of administrative experience, but it was tested in the classroom on a daily basis. I was also involved in a number of campus-wide initiatives to get faculty members discussing their innovations in teaching. There were faculty discussion groups on video-games and student motivation; understanding student misconceptions about science; syllabus design; and a group that organized forums for faculty members to present new ideas about teaching to their peers.

---

[81] It is unusual for someone who has been in a university's central administration to be elected to lead the Faculty Senate. Typically, these groups have an adversarial relationship as the Faculty Senate is charged with representing faculty values and the administration must mediate between pressures from the faculty and all other constituent groups.

INDEX

D

E

intrinsic rewards/feedback, xi, 23, 24, 27, 28, 65, 68, 71, 80, 81, 83, 92, 108, 118, 130, 136, 137, 138
introductory course, 105, 106, 107, 184
intuition, 39, 44
issue, The, 36, 37, 38, 42, 58, 59, 96, 120, 148

J

Jefferson, Thomas, 13, 111, 156
jigsaw puzzles, 65, 136
journal groups, 113, 114, 116, 119
Junto, The, 116

K

Keats, John, 50
King, Jr, Martin Luther, 157

L

law school students, 25
leadership, vii, 3, 4, 102, 114, 118, 122, 155, 156, 157, 158, 159, 160, 162, 164, 170, 172, 174, 175, 177, 178, 181
learned helplessness, 70
learner-centered syllabus, 139
learning environment, 33, 95, 119, 141, 175, 180
learning management system, 29, 98, 108, 109
lecture, 1, 2, 5, 6, 8, 12, 20, 29, 36, 67, 73, 74, 75, 78, 79, 87, 88, 90, 91, 92, 93, 94, 95, 96, 98, 99, 100, 101, 106, 119, 121, 129, 131, 142, 143, 144, 145, 146, 147, 149, 151, 160, 165, 184
leveled, 39, 56
liberal education, x, 15, 16, 20, 28, 58, 60, 78, 83, 84, 85, 156, 172, 173, 178, 180
liberal science and arts education, 15, 16, 104, 161
liberal-arts universities, 95
lighting, 151, 152

Lincoln, Abraham, 151
lived experiences, 39, 43
Locke, John, 13
logical fallacies, 36, 48, 96, 119
loose seating, 142
low-technology, 146

M

Machiavelli, 3, 157, 176
magic, 52, 60, 171
manageable risks, 81
mass practice, 68
massive open online classes, 97
medical school students, 25
medieval university, 8
mental filing cabinet, 19, 20, 21, 65, 87
mentor(s), 21, 88, 99, 120, 121, 122, 124, 126, 128, 158, 159, 175
Merrill Act, 129
meta-analysis, 90
metacognition, 35
Mile's Law, 56
minecraft, 77, 177
misconceptions about learning, 63, 65
modality, 68
Moses, 94
motivation, 13, 23, 28, 68, 77, 79, 115, 116, 128, 172, 177, 178, 186
Motor Club, The, 114, 116, 119
movie projector, 97
multitasking, 70
murder mystery, 161
music, xii, 28, 35, 63, 70, 97, 122, 131, 133, 136

N

near transfer, 21, 68, 83, 92
neurological control of movement, 114
Newton, Isaac, 65
North American house hippopotamus, 58

O

objective-question, 110
office hours, 122, 145
one-on-one, 30, 121, 122, 123, 170
online education, 97, 98
online examination, 109
operational definition, 45, 46
orthodontics, 2, 184
out-of-class learning, 122

P

parents, 16, 20, 42, 58, 98, 103, 123, 129, 162
Paris, 40, 45
passion, 9, 78, 99, 101, 102, 107, 120, 130, 135, 162, 164, 186
patternicity, 54, 55
Paul, Annie Murphy, 98, 99
peanut butter, 50, 64
pedagogy, 25, 116, 157, 173, 180
peer-reviewed journals, 124
peers, xii, 20, 53, 93, 123, 126, 144, 146, 187
perfect solution fallacy, 48
Philadelphia, 116
physical sciences, 26, 45, 183
physician, 41, 44
Plato, 34, 175
podium, 149, 151
poetic magic, 52, 53
pointification, 80
political discussions, 118
politicians, 14, 42, 95, 103, 104, 121, 157
post hoc, ergo propter hoc fallacy, 49
PowerPoint, 100
prehistoric ancestors, 29
prehistoric savannah, 53
primary sources, 11, 39, 41, 137
problem-solving, 65, 74, 88, 128, 129
procedural learning, 76
procrastinate, 64
professional meritocracy, 163

programmed textbooks, 97
proseminar, 114, 115
provost, x, 9, 100, 101, 103, 115, 139, 145, 183, 185, 186
psychology, 45, 56, 106, 115, 169, 171, 172, 173, 175, 176, 177, 181, 183
public speaking, 94
puzzles, 22, 66, 67, 68, 69, 73, 79, 85, 92, 130

Q

quadrivium, 161
questionable authority, 39, 42, 49

R

reasons, The, 2, 3, 36, 37, 38, 80, 89, 90, 91, 96, 101, 160
red herring fallacy, 49, 119, 174
reflective practice, x, 27, 28, 29, 30, 31, 33, 35, 36, 46, 47, 60, 66, 68, 70, 74, 79, 85, 88, 89, 90, 91, 92, 96, 101, 107, 110, 111, 113, 114, 120, 125, 126, 128, 129, 130, 131, 136, 138, 141, 146, 155, 158, 165, 167, 170, 176, 181
reflective thinking, 35
repetition, xii, 68, 100, 101, 145
replicate a research project, 126
research university, 8, 9, 10, 90, 123, 171
results from research, 38
reverberation, 150, 153
reward-system principle, 76
risk-taking principle, 76, 82
roving leaders, 155

S

saber-tooth cat, 53
Sample, Steven, 3
scholarly, ix, x, 6, 11, 17, 21, 33, 35, 39, 40, 41, 42, 45, 46, 50, 53, 56, 60, 61, 63, 64, 67, 75, 90, 100, 106, 107, 108, 114, 116,

T

U